GOOD VIBES BAKING

GOOD VIBES BAKING

Bakes To Make Your Soul *Shine*
and Your Taste Buds *Sing*

Sandro Farmhouse

Feel ↳ the Vibe

This book is a representation of why I love to bake. Baking has been a part of my life and journey since I was a child, and now to have a career doing something I love is everything.

I wanted to start this book with gratitude. Firstly, I want to say thank you to everyone who has supported me before, throughout, and after *The Great British Bake Off*. There's no way I would have got this far without the support I've received, and I am beyond grateful for it. Secondly, I want to thank you for buying this book. It means the world to me that you have faith in my recipes and want to support a new author, so a big thank you to you.

I wanted to write this book because it's always been a dream of mine and I never thought I'd have this opportunity. It's such a great way for me to connect with you all. I want you to feel as though you are baking beside me when you're using this book—I want you to feel the vibes and enjoy knowing that these recipes were created solely to make you feel good.

My baking journey started in my mum's kitchen. I can remember waking up to the smell of freshly baked cakes and going downstairs to lick the batter off the spoon. I was definitely more into the eating part than the baking part until I was a teenager and started baking my own cakes—dry cakes, sometimes hard as a rock and with no filling, but I still ate them all. Baking had become my passion.

Years later, when I lost my father, I remember being told the news and (for some weird reason) I went straight back home, baked a cake using a store-bought mix, filled and frosted it (again, using store-bought chocolate frosting), and then made loads of red roses using fondant. It was so therapeutic and that's when I realized I'd found my safety in baking.

Whenever I am going through anything, whether it's good or bad, I turn to baking. It's my way of expressing myself, and what a great way it is when you can then eat something delicious as well—it's a win-win situation. I pour my feelings into my bakes, feel better or lighter as a result, and I continue to build on my baking skills. And it feels good.

My baking journey has been mostly trial and error, learning from my (many) mistakes, to create some amazing cakes. I can proudly say that I am a self-taught baker and it hasn't always gone right. I've learned resilience, and that practice, practice, practice makes perfect. And without it all I wouldn't have reached the final of *The Great British Bake Off*. To be a part of such an amazing show, to be among such brilliant bakers, and to be judged by cooking icons was a dream with a cherry on top. I will forever be grateful!

Let's be real, life isn't always easy, but I find that baking can be so helpful. Not only is it fun and a great life skill, but I truly believe in its benefits for our mental well-being. I use baking as a type of therapy, just having a moment to myself in the kitchen, whether I've got music playing or *Real Housewives* in the background, I'm able to focus on my bake and giving myself a break.

People are always saying to me that baking is "hard," or "too much of a science," and my response is always, "it's only cake!" As long as you're having a good time making it (and it's edible, of course) then it's a good job done. Remember: in this kitchen, it's all about the vibe. That's what baking is all about for me. It's about going into your kitchen, putting on your favorite playlist, baking away, and letting all your worries and stresses just disappear for a good moment.

The chapters have been broken down into feelings rather than the more usual different types of bakes, or techniques to master. I wanted to have it this way to illustrate how the varying emotions we feel can help us connect a feeling to a particular bake.

Starting with Love Language, these bakes are some of my favorite ways to tell someone I love them. Imagine how you feel if your partner, a housemate, or a family member brings you something freshly baked—that's what it's all about. Next, in Give Me Confidence, it's all about taking a few challenges. You know those recipes that you look at in a book and wonder if you can do that? YASSS you can! And then sometimes there are those other days. You know those rainy days, when you're like "bleurgh" and you don't want to get out of bed? I've got just what you need to Lift Your Spirits. The next chapter, Touch the Sky, is all about the showstoppers. If you know me then you know I love to go BIG with my bakes, from tall, layered cakes, and beautiful decorations to even making your own wedding cake (see page 104). It's a Fiesta is all about what you're bringing to the party. If you want to be a bit more low key, then Sharing Is Caring is for you. These are recipes created to share with your neighbors, your colleagues, or your family, bringing your beautiful bakes to put a smile on people's faces. And finally, we have Many Hands. Baking is a bonding experience, and I love getting some friends over to get creative with me in the kitchen. My vibe is always about spreading joy.

And now, I'm so excited to have you join me in this journey. The world can be so hectic and loud, and I want to invite you to a quieter place where it's just you, this book, and whatever you choose to bake. Is there a better way to feel the vibe? And a tip for the road for anyone starting their baking journey: don't be so hard on yourself—the best way to learn is to make mistakes.

Enjoy yourself, and feel the vibe x

LOVE
LANGUAGE

One of my love languages is food. I think the quickest way to anyone's heart is by feeding them.

I had to have this as my first chapter in the book. It's something that screams "SANDRO." I love hosting and inviting friends over, and providing the best baked spread ever. It's something that truly makes me feel good, and that—let's be honest—is what it's all about: feeling good. In this chapter you will find lots of recipes to warm up anyone's heart, what better way to tell someone you love them than with a Giant Heart Cookie (see page 15) or a Chocolate Truffle Box (see page 28).

STRAWBERRY VANILLA PANCAKES

Makes 12

I love pancakes, as you might be able to tell throughout the book. This recipe is super easy to make, and serving it with some fresh strawberries (and maybe in bed) just takes it to a new level. Who wouldn't want to wake up to this?

1. Start with the strawberry coulis. Add the strawberries, lemon juice, powdered sugar, and vanilla paste to a pan and heat on medium. Bring to a boil and let it bubble and reduce down until thickened slightly and jammy, about 10–15 minutes. Taste for sweetness; depending on the season, you may need to add slightly more sugar. Set aside to cool completely (spreading it out on a plate or tray speeds up the cooling process).

2. To make your cream, whisk together the whipping cream, powdered sugar, and vanilla paste until soft peaks form. When the coulis has cooled, fold half of it through the cream to make beautiful strawberry streaks.

3. For your pancakes, start by separating the eggs. In a stand mixer (or mixing bowl with a handheld electric whisk), add the egg whites and whip until thick, fluffy, and forming stiff peaks. Set aside.

4. Pop the egg yolks in a separate bowl, with the flour, baking powder, salt, baking soda, sugar, and milk. Whisk until combined, then drizzle in the melted butter. Fold in one-third of the egg whites to loosen the mixture, then fold in the rest carefully, keeping as much air in the batter as possible.

5. Heat a nonstick skillet with a blob of butter and wipe around with a paper towel to remove the excess. Add a ladleful of pancake batter and let cook for 2–3 minutes until bubbles appear all over the surface. Flip it over and cook for another couple of minutes, then remove from the pan and wrap in a kitchen towel to keep warm while you cook the rest of the pancakes.

6. To serve, add three pancakes per person to a plate, as a stack or however you like. Drizzle the remaining coulis over, add swooshes of the cream, stud with some fresh strawberries, and then finish with some mint or basil leaves. No one will tell you off for adding a little maple syrup, too, if you like!

FOR THE STRAWBERRY COULIS

14oz (400g) strawberries, hulled and halved
juice of 1 lemon
scant 1½ cups (150g) powdered sugar, or to taste
1 tbsp vanilla paste

FOR THE CREAM

1¼ cups (300ml) whipping cream
scant 1 cup (100g) powdered sugar
1 tbsp vanilla paste

FOR THE PANCAKES

4 large eggs
1¾ cups (225g) all-purpose flour
2½ tsp baking powder
½ tsp salt
½ tsp baking soda
1 tbsp sugar
scant 1 cup (225ml) whole milk
3½ tbsp (50g) unsalted butter, melted, plus extra for frying

TO SERVE

7oz (200g) strawberries, hulled and quartered
mint or basil leaves
maple syrup (optional)

GIANT HEART COOKIE

Serves 12

Cookies in any form are my favorite bakes. This giant heart cookie is one to share. It's so cute, you can decorate it or write a message with some icing on top to brighten up anyone's day.

1. Preheat the oven to 350°F (180°C).

2. Beat the butter, sugar, and light brown sugar together until smooth, and then add the egg. Sift together the flour, baking soda, baking powder, and salt, then add the dry ingredients to the butter, sugar, and egg mixture. Mix gently until a soft dough is formed.

3. Fold in the rolled oats, pistachios, white chocolate, and raspberries.

4. Break off pieces of the dough and gently push them into the lined pan, leveling it out to make a smooth cookie.

5. Bake for 20–25 minutes if using freeze-dried raspberries, or 25–30 minutes if using frozen raspberries, or until golden brown.

6. Leave to cool in the pan for 20 minutes, or until set, and then transfer to a wire rack to cool completely. Add the extra raspberries and pistachios for decoration across the top, and share the love with your friends, family, or that special someone!

½ cup plus 2½ tbsp (150g) unsalted butter
½ cup (100g) sugar
½ cup (100g) light brown sugar
1 large egg, beaten
1¾ cups (240g) all-purpose flour
½ tsp baking soda
½ tsp baking powder
¼ tsp fine sea salt
1 cup (100g) rolled oats
10½oz (300g) pistachios, shelled and roughly chopped (5½oz/150g shelled and chopped weight), plus ¾oz (20g) for decoration
9oz (250g) white chocolate, roughly chopped
1¾oz (50g) freeze-dried raspberries or 5½oz (150g) frozen raspberries, plus ¾oz (20g) broken up for decoration

shallow 9in (22cm) heart-shaped springform or loose-bottom cake pan, greased and lined

CHOCOLATE, COCONUT & CHERRY DESSERT

Serves 6

FOR THE COCONUT CAKE

2½oz (75g) dried, shredded coconut
½ cup plus 1 tbsp (125g) unsalted
  butter, softened
½ cup plus 2 tbsp (125g) sugar
2 large eggs
scant 1 cup (125g) all-purpose flour,
  sifted
1 tsp baking powder
¼ tsp salt

FOR THE CHOCOLATE MOUSSE

5½oz (150g) dark chocolate
  (minimum 72% cocoa solids)
3 very fresh large eggs (they'll be raw)
1 tsp sugar
⅔ cup (150ml) whipping cream

FOR THE CHERRY COMPOTE

14oz (400g) jar cherry jam
  or compote
2 tsp brandy

FOR THE TOPPING

⅔ cup (150ml) whipping cream
6 cherries with stems (if in season;
  you can also spray with gold dust
  or brush on gold leaf if you like)
6 mint sprigs (if no fresh cherries)

*8 in (20 cm) square cake pan,
greased and lined
6 glasses or small bowls*

A quick and easy version of a Black Forest cake, this is one of those desserts that looks beautiful served in individual glasses.

1. Preheat the oven to 350°F (180°C).

2. Start by making the cake. Toast the coconut in a dry skillet for a couple of minutes until golden, then pour out onto a plate to cool.

3. Cream together the butter and sugar until super light and fluffy, about 3–4 minutes. Add the toasted coconut and then beat in the eggs, one at a time. Fold through the flour, baking powder, and salt.

4. Transfer the batter to the lined cake pan and bake for about 15–18 minutes until lightly golden and a skewer comes out clean. Allow it to cool in the pan while you make the chocolate mousse.

5. Melt the chocolate at 30-second intervals in the microwave, stirring well after each blast, until melted completely (it usually takes about 1 minute 30 seconds). Separate the eggs and then stir the yolks through the chocolate.

6. Put the egg whites in a clean bowl and, using a handheld electric whisk, whip the egg whites until soft peaks form. Add the sugar and continue to whisk until glossy. Transfer to another bowl and set aside.

7. Back in the mixing bowl (no need to wash!) whip the cream until soft peaks form. Pour in the melted chocolate and egg yolks, and slowly whisk until combined. Fold through the egg whites.

8. To jazz up the store-bought jam or compote, stir in the brandy.

9. Whip the whipping cream for the topping until soft peaks form.

10. Turn out the cooled cake and use the glasses to cut out six circles of cake (keep the scraps). Slice each circle in half across its middle to create 12 thin slices of cake.

11. Add some of the cake scraps to the bottom of each glass to create an even base, then add a layer of cherry compote followed by some chocolate mousse. Add a circle of cake to each glass and repeat the layers of compote and mousse. Add the final layer of cake, compote, and mousse, and finish with a swoop of whipped cream. Chill for an hour. Add the cherry or a mint sprig just before serving!

BROWNIE & STRAWBERRY COOKIES

Makes 12–15

Have you ever made brownies but can't be bothered to wait until it properly sets like a brownie should? Well, this is the faster alternative. It's gooey, fudgey, and chocolaty, and it is one of my faves.

1. Preheat the oven to 350°F (180°C).

2. In a small saucepan set over a low heat, melt the chocolate and butter, stirring well to avoid burning.

3. In a bowl, use a handheld electric whisk to whip up the sugar, light brown sugar, and eggs until doubled in size. Pour in the chocolate butter mix and whisk again. Sift in the flour, baking powder, and salt, and then fold gently.

4. Fold in most of the freeze-dried strawberries and chocolate chunks (save a handful of each).

5. Using an ice-cream scoop, pop dollops of cookie mix onto the lined baking sheets and flatten slightly, leaving a gap between each.

6. Bake for 12–15 minutes until set around the edges, then remove them from the oven and press the reserved freeze-dried strawberries and chocolate chunks into the tops.

7. Leave to cool on the baking sheets for an hour before enjoying.

6½oz (185g) dark chocolate
  (minimum 72% cocoa solids)
½ cup plus 2 tbsp (140g) unsalted
  butter
½ cup (100g) sugar
½ cup (100g) light brown sugar
2 large eggs
1 cup plus 2 tbsp (150g)
  all-purpose flour
1 tsp baking powder
½ tsp salt
1oz (30g) freeze-dried
  strawberry pieces
7oz (200g) dark chocolate chunks

2 baking sheets, lined

WHITE CHOCOLATE & RASPBERRY DESSERT POTS

Makes 4

FOR THE CRYSTALLIZED ROSE PETALS

1–2 roses, petals rinsed and dried
1 large egg white
½ cup (100g) sugar

FOR THE SHORTBREAD

3½ tbsp (50g) unsalted butter,
  cold and cubed
generous ⅓ cup (50g) all-purpose
  flour, plus extra for dusting
2 tsp ice-cold water
1 tbsp sugar

FOR THE RASPBERRY JELLY

2 sheets platinum-grade gelatin
10½oz (300g) fresh or frozen
  raspberries, plus extra
  to decorate
¼ cup (50g) sugar

FOR THE WHITE CHOCOLATE MOUSSE

9oz (250g) white chocolate
1¾ cups (400ml) whipping cream
2 sheets platinum-grade gelatin
4 large egg yolks
½ cup (100g) sugar

baking sheet, greased and lined
4 dessert glasses

This is an elegant dessert when you want to impress dinner guests.

1. We'll start with the crystallized rose petals. Brush each rose petal with some egg white and then sprinkle with sugar to coat. Leave to dry on a wire rack for 12–24 hours.

2. Preheat the oven to 350°F (180°C).

3. For the shortbread, add the butter and flour to a bowl and use your fingertips to rub them together. When it is like fine breadcrumbs, add the ice-cold water and the sugar, and bring it together to a dough.

4. Lightly flour a surface and roll out the dough to a big circle about ¼-in (5-mm) thick. Place on the parchment-lined baking sheet and bake for 10–12 minutes until golden at the edges. Allow to cool completely on the baking sheet. When cooled, crumble into small pieces and set aside.

5. For the jelly, break the gelatin sheets into pieces and pop in a large bowl, add a splash (approximately 2 tbsp) of cold water to cover, and allow to bloom for 5 minutes.

6. Add the raspberries and the sugar to a small saucepan, place over medium heat, and cook until the raspberries break down and release their juice, about 10 minutes. Allow to reduce slightly and then remove from the heat. Set aside for 5 minutes and then strain into the bowl with the gelatin. Press with a spoon to extract all the juice. Discard the seeds and pulp. Stir to combine well and then pour into the bottom of dessert glasses. Leave to set in the fridge for 2 hours.

7. To make the white chocolate mousse, add the chocolate and half of the cream to a large heatproof bowl set over a pan of simmering water and allow to melt, stirring occasionally. Leave to cool slightly.

8. Add the gelatin to another bowl with enough water to cover (approximately 2 tbsp), then allow it to soften.

9. In another heatproof bowl, whisk the egg yolks and sugar over a pan of simmering water until thick pale ribbons are made and the sugar has dissolved. Fold in the white chocolate cream mixture and the drained bloomed gelatin leaves. Let cool to room temperature.

10. Whisk the remaining whipping cream until soft peaks form and then fold into the cooled white chocolate mixture. Spoon into the dessert glasses and refrigerate for 2–3 hours until firm.

11. Decorate with a crumbling of shortbread, a few extra raspberries, and the crystallized rose petals.

RASPBERRY & LEMON ÉCLAIRS

Makes 8

FOR THE FILLING

5½oz (150g) raspberries
1 batch Thick Vanilla Pastry
 Cream (see page 196), cooled
dash pink gel or paste food
 coloring (optional)

FOR THE CHOUX PASTRY

3½ tbsp (50g) unsalted butter
½ cup (75g) white bread flour
¼ tsp salt
2 large eggs, beaten

FOR THE ICING

scant 1½ cups (150g)
 powdered sugar
juice of 1 lemon

TO DECORATE

freeze-dried raspberries
gold leaf
edible flowers

2 baking sheets, lined
2 large piping bags
large round nozzle
large star nozzle

One of my favorite things to eat is a freshly baked pastry and these éclairs are a classic. The flavor combo is one for everyone—even if you're not usually a fan of lemon, this éclair will convince you to think differently.

1. Start by making your pastry cream the day before and leaving it covered to set in the fridge.

2. To make the choux, to a small saucepan, add the butter and 6½ tablespoons (100ml) water and heat gently until the butter is melted. Bring to a boil and throw in all of the flour and salt. Beat well over a low heat for a couple of minutes more until the mixture is stiff and sticks well to itself.

3. Remove from the heat and beat for a minute to allow the mixture to cool. Add the eggs, a little at a time, while you continue to beat. You may not need all of the egg, but as soon as the mixture gets to dropping consistency (it drops off the spatula nicely), then the mix is ready. Leave to cool.

4. Preheat the oven to 400°F (200°C).

5. Put the cooled choux pastry into a large piping bag fitted with a large round nozzle. Pipe eight éclairs about 5 in (12 cm) in length over the two lined baking sheets, leaving plenty of room between each one for them to puff up.

6. Bake for 20–25 minutes, or until dark golden brown.

7. When the éclairs are done, poke a couple of small holes in the bottom of each one to release the steam and then leave to cool on a wire rack.

8. For the filling, puree the raspberries in a blender and then pass through a sieve to remove the seeds. Add to a bowl with the pastry cream and use a handheld electric whisk to beat them together until smooth and lighter in color. Add some food coloring if you'd like a pinker finish! Add the raspberry pastry cream to a piping bag fitted with a large star nozzle.

9. Slice each éclair in half lengthwise, then pipe waves of pastry cream along the bottom half.

10. Make the lemon icing by mixing together the powdered sugar and enough lemon juice to come to a thin icing consistency. Dip each top half in the icing and place on top of the filled bottom half.

11. To decorate, sprinkle over freeze-dried raspberries and gently brush on some gold leaf. Finish with edible flowers.

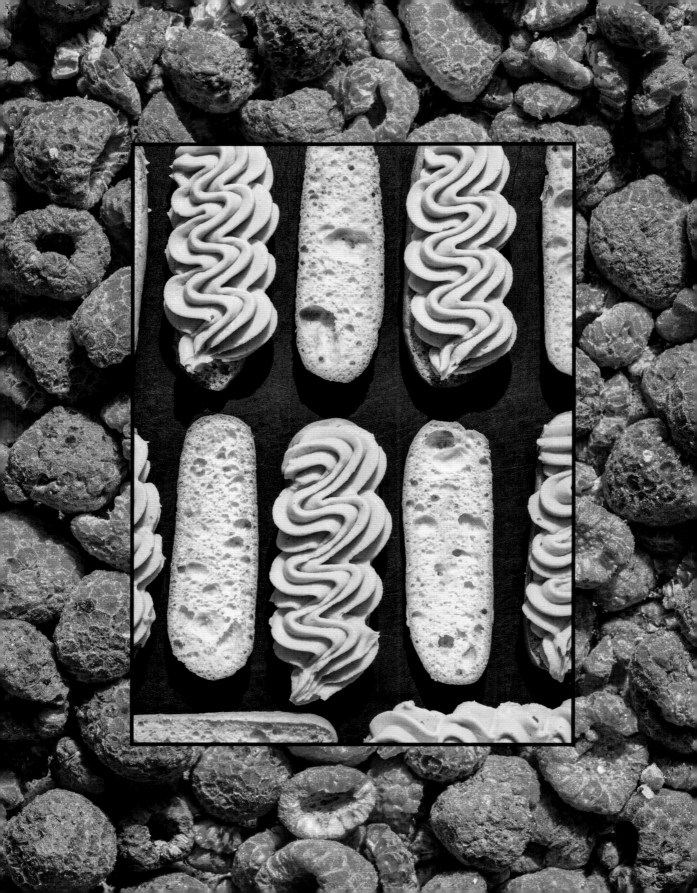

BLACK FOREST COOKIES

Makes 24

I just love the taste of a Black Forest cake (see page 16 for my Chocolate, Coconut, and Cherry Dessert), so here are those flavors in cookie form. These cookies have the sweetness of the cherries and the bitterness of the dark chocolate, and they are super fudgey and chunky—I'm obsessed.

1. Put the butter and chocolate in a heatproof bowl set over a pan of simmering water and allow to melt gently, stirring occasionally to help it along.

2. While that's on the go, add the sugar, light brown sugar, and eggs to a bowl and use a handheld electric whisk to whip them up for 5 minutes until doubled in size and pale.

3. Gently pour the melted butter and sugar mixture into the bowl, along with the 3½ tablespoons (50ml) kirsch, and whisk again.

4. Sift in the flour, baking powder, baking soda, and salt, and fold through carefully, trying not to lose any air. Finally, stir the cherries and white chocolate into the dough.

5. Use an ice cream scoop or spoon to make around 24 cookies on the parchment-lined baking sheets, spacing them out well, as they spread quite a lot. Pop these into the fridge for 40 minutes.

6. Preheat the oven to 350°F (180°C).

7. Bake the cookies for 10–12 minutes, or until set around the edges.

8. Spritz the tops of the cookies with the extra kirsch for a burst of flavor and leave to cool completely on the baking sheets. Enjoy with a cherry cocktail if you like!

½ cup plus 1 tbsp (125g) unsalted butter
6½oz (185g) dark chocolate (minimum 72% cocoa solids)
½ cup (100g) sugar
½ cup (100g) light brown sugar
2 large eggs
3½ tbsp (50ml) kirsch, plus 1½ tbsp (25ml) in a small spray bottle
1½ cups (200g) all-purpose flour
1 tsp baking powder
½ tsp baking soda
¼ tsp fine sea salt
5½oz (150g) Amarena cherries, drained (keep the syrup for cocktails!)
5½oz (150g) white chocolate, roughly chopped

2 baking sheets, lined

NUTTY CARAMEL CUPCAKES

Makes 12

Rich chocolate cupcakes topped with salted caramel buttercream and finished with crunchy peanuts and a sprinkle of salt—this recipe is a banger!

1. Preheat the oven to 350°F (180°C).

2. For the cupcakes, beat together the butter, dark brown sugar, and sugar until super light and fluffy, about 4–5 minutes.

3. Mix the instant coffee granules with the hot water and half the cocoa powder in a mug to make a paste, and then beat this into the cupcake mixture.

4. Beat in the eggs, one at a time, and then fold in the flour, baking powder, and salt in two batches, followed by the remaining cocoa powder. Divide the batter evenly among the cupcake cases.

5. Bake for 18–20 minutes until well risen and a skewer inserted into the middle comes out clean.

6. Allow to cool in the pan for 10 minutes, before transferring the cupcakes to a wire rack to cool completely.

7. For the buttercream, add the softened butter to a stand mixer fitted with the paddle attachment (or use a mixing bowl and handheld electric whisk) and beat until pale and fluffy. Add the powdered sugar in two batches, sifting in well, and then beat for 5–8 minutes until super pale and fluffy. Add half the salted caramel (around 1 cup/250g) and beat to combine. Pop into a piping bag with a nozzle of your choice.

8. When the cakes are cool, use a small pointed knife to cut out a 1-inch circle in the top of each cupcake. Remove and then fill with some of the remaining salted caramel, popping the cake back on top.

9. Using a circular motion, pipe the salted caramel buttercream onto the cupcakes, making sure you cover the middle. Decorate with a sprinkling of peanuts, a slice of peanut caramel chocolate bar, and a pinch of flaky sea salt.

FOR THE CUPCAKES

½ cup plus 4 tbsp (175g) unsalted
  butter, softened
½ cup plus 2 tbsp (125g) dark
  brown sugar
¼ cup (50g) sugar
1 tsp instant coffee granules
2 tbsp hot water
½ cup (50g) cocoa powder
3 large eggs
1⅓ cups (175g) all-purpose flour
1½ tsp baking powder
¼ tsp salt

FOR THE SALTED CARAMEL BUTTERCREAM

1 cup (225g) unsalted butter,
  softened
3¼ cups (450g) powdered sugar
1 batch Salted Caramel, cooled
  (see page 199)

TO DECORATE

1¾oz (50g) roasted salted
  peanuts, roughly chopped
1 peanut caramel chocolate bar,
  cut into 12 slices
flaky sea salt

*12-hole cupcake pan, lined
with cupcake cases
piping bag
nozzle of your choice*

CHOCOLATE TRUFFLE BOX

Makes 32

All the best gifts are homemade, and this makes a lovely one. Scrunch up a large square of parchment paper and place it in a gift box. Place the truffles in mini cupcake cases and arrange on top.

1. In a small saucepan over medium heat, heat the cream, butter, and flavoring together, and gently bring the mixture to just below a boil.

2. Pop the chocolate in a large mixing bowl and then pour the hot cream mixture over the top of the chocolate. Leave to stand for 2 minutes, then stir well to combine. Pour into the plastic-wrap-lined loaf pan, wrap to cover the top, and refrigerate for 4 hours or overnight.

3. Turn out the block of truffle, peel off the plastic wrap, and slice it into 32 cubes. Dust them in the cocoa powder or sprinkle them with assorted toppings.

4. Pop into mini cupcake cases and serve on a platter after dinner, or arrange in a gift box for friends.

FOR THE TRUFFLES

1 cup (250ml) whipping cream
1½ tbsp (20g) unsalted butter
2 tsp liqueur or flavoring of
  your choice (mint, orange zest,
  kirsch, etc.)
9oz (250g) dark chocolate,
  roughly chopped

TO DECORATE

cocoa powder
chopped nuts
freeze-dried raspberries
dried, shredded coconut
crushed chocolate sandwich
  cookies

*2lb (900g) loaf pan, lined with
plastic wrap
32 mini cupcake cases*

CHOCOLATE HAZELNUT LAYERED CAKE

Serves 12

FOR THE ROASTED HAZELNUTS

9oz (250g) blanched hazelnuts

FOR THE HAZELNUT CAKE

1 cup (220g) unsalted
  butter, softened
1 cup plus 2 tbsp (220g) sugar
1 tsp vanilla bean paste
4 large eggs
1 cup plus 2 tbsp (150g)
  all-purpose flour
2 tsp baking powder
¼ tsp salt
scant 1¼ cup (120g)
  ground almonds

FOR THE CHOCOLATE CAKE

½ cup (50g) cocoa powder
1 tsp instant coffee granules
6–8 tbsp hot water
1 cup plus 2 tbsp (250g) unsalted
  butter, softened
½ cup (100g) light brown sugar
¾ cup (150g) sugar
4 large eggs
1¾ cups plus 2 tbsp (250g) flour
2½ tsp baking powder
½ tsp baking soda
¾ tsp fine sea salt

You know those little round chocolate balls with hazelnuts? Well, this is the cake version. I love this cake; it's so tasty with the crunchiness of the hazelnuts, the sweetness of the chocolate ganache, and the softest cake ever. I mean, what else can I say to convince you to make it? If you have any ganache left over at the end, pop it in the fridge to harden, before rolling into balls to make your own hazelnut truffles.

1. Preheat the oven to 350°F (180°C).

2. Start by making the roasted hazelnuts. Add the hazelnuts to a baking sheet and roast for 5–8 minutes until golden brown. Leave to cool completely and then chop finely. Set aside.

3. For the hazelnut cake, beat together the butter, sugar, and vanilla bean paste until pale and fluffy. Add the eggs, one at a time, beating well after each one. Sift in the flour, baking powder, and salt, and then fold these in gently with the ground almonds. Fold through 5½oz (150g) of the cooled and chopped roasted hazelnuts.

4. Divide the batter between the prepared cake pans and bake for 25–30 minutes until risen and a skewer inserted into the middle comes out clean.

5. Allow to cool in the pans for 10 minutes before tipping out onto a wire rack to cool completely. Grease and reline your pans again with parchment paper to be ready for the chocolate cakes.

6. To make the chocolate cake, whisk together the cocoa powder, coffee granules, and enough of the hot water in a small bowl to make a smooth paste. Beat the butter, light brown sugar, and sugar together until lighter in color, and then add the eggs, one at a time, as before. Add the chocolate and coffee mix, and then sift in the flour, baking powder, baking soda, and salt, and fold through.

7. Divide between the two pans again and bake for 25–30 minutes until risen and a skewer inserted into the middle comes out clean.

8. Allow to cool in the tins for 10 minutes before tipping out onto a wire rack to cool completely.

9. To make the chocolate hazelnut buttercream, beat the chocolate hazelnut spread into the Vanilla Buttercream and put most of it in a large piping bag (reserving some for the decoration). Snip off the tip and leave at room temperature.

10. To make the hazelnut ganache, heat the cream in the microwave for 1–2 minutes until just below boiling. Add the chopped chocolate, chocolate hazelnut spread, and the remaining 3½oz (100g) chopped roasted hazelnuts to a bowl, and pour over the hot cream. Leave to stand for 2 minutes before stirring to mix evenly.

11. To assemble, level each cake with a serrated knife to make them easier to stack. Pipe a circle of buttercream around three of the cake layers and fill the circles with a layer of hazelnut ganache.

FOR THE CHOCOLATE HAZELNUT BUTTERCREAM

7oz (200g) chocolate hazelnut
   spread
1 batch Vanilla Buttercream
   (see page 196)

FOR THE HAZELNUT GANACHE

¾ cup (175ml) whipping cream
3½oz (100g) dark chocolate,
   chopped
3½oz (100g) chocolate hazelnut
   spread

FOR THE CHOCOLATE DRIP

scant 1 cup (200ml) whipping
   cream
3½oz (100g) dark chocolate,
   chopped

TO DECORATE

6 chocolate and hazelnut truffles

*2 (6 in/15 cm) round cake pans,
greased and lined
2 piping bags
star nozzle*

12. Stack the cake layers, alternately in flavor, putting the unfrosted layer on top. Crumb-coat the outside with more of the buttercream and pop in the fridge for 1 hour or the freezer for 30 minutes.

13. When the crumb coat is totally cold, frost the cake with the remaining buttercream in the piping bag, making it as smooth or as textured as you wish.

14. To make the ganache for the chocolate drip, heat the cream in the microwave for 1–2 minutes until just below boiling. Add the chocolate to a bowl, pour over the cream, and leave to stand for 2 minutes before stirring to mix evenly.

15. Slowly pour the ganache on top of the cake and use the back of a spoon to force the ganache to run down the side of the cake to create the drip effect. If you find that you need more ganache in some areas, pour a little extra close to the area you want the drips. Place it back in the fridge or freezer to set the ganache.

16. Transfer the reserved buttercream to a piping bag fitted with a star nozzle and pipe 6 rosettes around the top of the cake, topping each with a truffle.

GIVE ME
CONFIDENCE

Let me tell you, if you can bake the recipes in this chapter, you can bake anything.

If you can't, I give you full license to come back to this chapter at a later date! Confidence, not just in baking but in yourself, can take you to new places. It's something that can be nurtured. I'm all about confidence now, but I haven't always been that way. At school I was bullied, so having lots of confidence now is all down to work—telling myself I'm good enough and truly believing it. It has really changed my life. I hope this chapter not only makes you feel differently about baking if you are scared, but might also inspire you to be confident in your everyday life. If you're not feeling confident straight away, why not try the Boozy Tiramisu Dessert (see page 47) before you work up to something like the Key Lime Pie Deux Mille Feuille (see page 52).

RAINBOW CRÊPE CAKE

Serves 8

We are all nervous when it comes to making crêpes, but, I'm telling you it's so easy. I avoided making them for ages, but when I finally did, I realized it was beyond easy ... so why not make them into a rainbow cake?

1. Add the flour, sugar, and salt to a bowl and make a well in the center. Add the eggs and egg yolk, and whisk slowly to start. Slowly add the milk in a steady stream, whisking in one direction only to avoid lumps. Stir in the melted butter and let the batter rest for 2 hours in the fridge, if you have time (resting helps create a smoother batter and lighter pancakes, but isn't essential if time is short).

2. After the resting time, split the batter among six bowls and color each one a different shade to make a rainbow. You can make them as pastel or as vibrant as you like.

3. Heat a large skillet over medium heat and brush with oil. Ladle half of one of the pancake batters in and swirl around to make a thin crêpe. Cook on low for 2 minutes on each side until the edges just begin to turn golden, being careful not to let it brown too much, as this will impact the color. You should get two crêpes out of each color, so 12 in total. Leave to cool with a sheet of parchment paper between each one.

4. To assemble the cake, whisk the whipping cream and powdered sugar together until soft peaks form. Add one violet crêpe to the serving plate and spread evenly with about 2–3 heaped tablespoons of cream. Top with the other violet crêpe and spread with more cream. Repeat the crêpe and cream layers, working through the rainbow colors, finishing with red on the top.

5. Add a final layer of whipped cream and decorate with a circle of fruit, arranged in rainbow order, too, if you fancy!

FOR THE CRÊPES

1¾ cups (230g) all-purpose flour
2 tbsp (25g) sugar
pinch salt
2 large eggs
1 large egg yolk
2¼ cups (550ml) whole milk
3½ tbsp (50g) unsalted butter, melted
red, orange, yellow, green, blue, and violet gel food coloring
vegetable oil, for frying

TO ASSEMBLE

2½ cups (600ml) whipping cream
scant 1 cup (100g) powdered sugar
fresh fruit of your choice

CRÈME BRÛLÉE DOUGHNUTS

Makes 12

FOR THE DOUGH

scant ⅔ cup (140ml) whole milk
3½ tbsp (50g) unsalted butter
2 cups (300g) white bread flour
4 tsp (20g) sugar
1 (¼oz/7g) packet fast acting
  dried yeast
1 large egg, beaten
about 2 cups (500ml) vegetable or
  sunflower oil, for deep-frying

FOR THE CRÈME LÉGÈRE

⅔ cup (150ml) whipping cream
1 batch Thick Vanilla Pastry
  Cream (see page 196), cooled

FOR THE CARAMEL

1¾ cups (350g) sugar

2 baking sheets, lined
piping bag
long nozzle

I love a doughnut—it must be one of my favorite things to eat. Tearing into that soft dough to find a tasty filling ... just the thought is making me salivate! And these doughnuts, with the caramel top and the vanilla cream filling ... well, all I can say is, you're welcome.

1. In a small bowl, microwave the milk and butter until the butter has melted and the milk is slightly warm.

2. Add the flour, sugar, and yeast to a mixer fitted with a dough hook (or use a mixing bowl and work by hand) and make a well in the center. Add the warmed milk and start to combine slowly. When combined, add the egg and then knead for 8–10 minutes until a soft dough forms that springs back when poked.

3. Cover with a kitchen towel or lightly greased plastic wrap and leave in a warm place for 1½–2 hours until doubled in size.

4. When risen, knock back the dough and divide into 12 balls. Pop onto the parchment-lined baking sheets and cover with a kitchen towel again to rise for another hour.

5. Heat the oil in a large saucepan to 320°F (160°C). While the oil is heating, pat the dough balls gently to flatten them slightly.

6. Fry 2–3 doughnuts at a time, flipping them over after a minute or when golden brown to cook the other side. Use a slotted spoon to transfer them to a wire rack set over a baking sheet and leave to cool for 30 minutes.

7. For the crème légère, whip the cream until soft peaks form and then fold through the pastry cream. Pop into a piping bag fitted with a long nozzle.

8. Poke a hole into each doughnut and carefully squeeze the crème légère into the doughnuts.

9. For the caramel, in a small saucepan, heat the sugar gently over a low heat with a splash (approximately 1 tbsp) of water until the sugar has dissolved. Increase the heat and allow to bubble. Let caramelize until it's a deep golden brown and then remove it from the heat.

10. Pour the caramel carefully over the doughnuts, letting the caramel drip down the sides. Leave to harden for 15 minutes.

Boston Cream Variation: simply top with chocolate ganache instead of the caramel!

Brandy Salted Caramel Variation: use the Salted Caramel recipe on page 199, adding 2 teaspoons brandy to the caramel and piping this into the middle of the doughnuts along with the vanilla crème légère above.

BLUEBERRY CINNAMON ROLLS

Makes 12

FOR THE DOUGH

3 cups (400g) whole wheat
  bread flour
1 (¼oz/7g) packet fast acting
  dried yeast
1 tsp salt
3¼ tbsp (40g) light brown sugar
2 tbsp (30g) unsalted butter,
  softened
scant 1 cup (200ml) whole milk,
  microwaved for 30 seconds to
  take the chill off
1 large egg, beaten

FOR THE FILLING

½ cup plus 6 tbsp (200g) unsalted
  butter, softened
3 tsp ground cinnamon
6½ tbsp (80g) light brown sugar
9oz (250g) blueberries

FOR THE ICING

7oz (200g) cream cheese
scant 1 cup (100g) powdered
  sugar
3½ tbsp (50g) unsalted butter,
  softened
1 tbsp poppy seeds

*13 x 9 in (33 x 23 cm) baking
dish or roasting pan, buttered*

If you want to fill your home with the luxurious smell of cinnamon, get a batch of these rolls in the oven!

1. Start with the dough. In a stand mixer fitted with a dough hook (or use a mixing bowl and work by hand), add the flour, yeast, salt, and light brown sugar. Mix to combine. Add the butter, milk, and egg, and allow it to come together into a dough. Knead in the stand mixer (or by hand) for about 7–10 minutes until a soft dough forms, which springs back when touched. Cover with plastic wrap and leave to rise for around 2 hours, or until doubled in size.

2. While the dough is rising, we'll make the filling. In a mixing bowl smush together the softened butter, cinnamon, and light brown sugar until smooth. Leave at room temperature until you're ready to roll.

3. Divide the blueberries in half. Finely chop half of them and leave the rest whole.

4. Knock back the risen dough and then roll it out to a rectangle, 10 x 14 in (25 x 35 cm). Spread the cinnamon filling over the dough using a spatula or the back of a spoon. Sprinkle over the chopped blueberries, followed by the whole ones.

5. Roll up the dough from one of the long ends to create a sausage shape. Cut it into 12 even pieces. Push in any blueberries poking out of the rolls so they don't burn.

6. Nestle them together in the buttered dish or pan and then leave to prove for a further 45 minutes. Preheat the oven to 375°F (190°C) when you have 15 minutes left on the proving time.

7. Bake the rolls for 20–25 minutes and leave to cool in the dish.

8. Make the icing by beating together the cream cheese, powdered sugar, and softened butter, and then swoosh or drizzle it over the cinnamon rolls. Sprinkle over the poppy seeds, then tear and share!

BUTTER-SCOTCH BURNED BUTTER CRÊPES

Serves 4

FOR THE BUTTERSCOTCH SAUCE

¾ cup (150g) light brown sugar
1 tbsp molasses
1 tbsp light corn syrup
2 tbsp (30g) unsalted butter
scant 1 cup (200ml) whipping
  cream

FOR THE CRÊPES

1 cup (250ml) whole milk
scant 1 cup (200ml) whipping
  cream
3 large eggs
3½ tbsp (50g) unsalted butter,
  melted, plus extra for cooking
1½ cups (185g) all-purpose flour

FOR THE BURNED BUTTER BANANAS

6½ tbsp (100g) unsalted butter
4 bananas, sliced in half
  lengthwise

TO SERVE (OPTIONAL)

vanilla ice cream

Have you ever had this combo on a crêpe? I bet not. It's the burned butter bananas with the butterscotch sauce for me. It makes them the tastiest crêpes I've ever made or eaten.

1. Start with the butterscotch sauce. In a heavy-bottomed saucepan add the light brown sugar, molasses, corn syrup, and 4 tablespoons water. Melt over low heat. Increase the heat to a bubble and let the sugar turn a dark amber. Take it further than you think because the cream really lightens it up. Off the heat, stir in the butter and whipping cream. Leave in the pan to warm through before serving.

2. For the crêpes, use an immersion blender to whiz all of the ingredients up in a large bowl. (Or whisk the wet into the dry with a hand whisk.)

3. Pop a large skillet over medium heat. Rub the pan with a little butter and then ladle in enough batter to thinly cover the center of the pan. Roll it around to reach the edges and cook for 2–3 minutes on each side until golden. Wrap in foil and set aside to keep warm while you make the rest (the batter should make eight crepes).

4. To make the burned butter bananas, add the butter to the same pan and let it froth and bubble until nutty and dark brown. Fry the bananas on each side for a couple of minutes until golden at the edges.

5. Serve two crêpes per plate, with the bananas across, a drizzle of the burned butter, and some butterscotch sauce. Vanilla ice cream is optional but DELISH.

BOOZY TIRAMISU DESSERT

Serves 6

If you know me, then you'll know my ultimate favorite dessert ever is a tiramisu. It's easy and beyond tasty. I made boozy miniature versions and they're so cute for a little night in with friends.

1. Add the Irish cream liqueur and coffee to a dish and break the ladyfingers in half. Dip each half into the mixture on both sides and then leave on a plate. Save the dipping liquid!

2. To make our super easy cream, add the whipping cream, mascarpone, powdered sugar, and vanilla paste to a bowl and beat until smooth and soft peaks form. Whisk in the reserved dipping liquid and then we are ready to layer up.

3. Add one half of a ladyfinger to the bottom of each glass, followed by a level spoonful of the cream. Dust over some cocoa powder and then repeat, adding more ladyfingers as you need to as the glass gets wider.

4. For the last layer, cut out six hearts of parchment paper and place on the cream layer. Dust the remaining cocoa powder over the top, followed by a grating of your favorite chocolate. Remove the heart stencils and let set in the fridge for 4 hours.

⅔ cup (150ml) Irish cream
  liqueur
3 shots fresh espresso
  (or 3 tbsp instant espresso
  made up with 5 tbsp/75ml
  boiling water), cooled
18 ladyfingers
1¼ cups (300ml) whipping cream
9oz (250g) mascarpone or
  cream cheese
scant 1 cup (100g) powdered
  sugar
1 tsp vanilla paste
2 tbsp cocoa powder
2 squares (approximately
  1oz/25g) chocolate (your fave
  kind!)

6 martini glasses

ESPRESSO MARTINI CHEESECAKE

Serves 8

This is my drink, so why not make it into a bake? I love anything coffee related, whether it's at a bar or in a bake—I just really love the taste.

1. Prepare the cake pan by wrapping it with two layers of thick foil, all the way up to the top edge. Preheat the oven to 375°F (190°C).

2. For the base, crush the speculoos cookies to a fine crumb and then stir through the melted butter. Press the cookie mixture into the springform pan pressing it up the sides of the pan. Bake in the oven for 10 minutes, and then set aside while you make the filling. Turn the oven down to 325°F (160°C).

3. In a small bowl, mix together the instant coffee granules and boiling water, and set aside to cool.

4. Using a stand mixer fitted with the paddle attachment (or a mixing bowl and handheld electric whisk), beat the cream cheese, flour, and light brown sugar together until fluffy, about 3–4 minutes.

5. In a bowl, whisk together the eggs, sour cream, coffee liqueur, and the cooled brewed coffee until smooth, and then slowly add this into the cream cheese mixture. Pour into the prepared pan.

6. Place the pan into a deep roasting pan in the oven and pour a kettle of boiling water into the roasting pan. Bake the cheesecake for 1 hour 10 minutes, or until the edges are set and the middle is still slightly wobbly.

7. Once done, put a wooden spoon in the oven door to keep it ajar and leave the cheesecake in the oven until the oven has cooled down completely, then transfer the pan to the fridge overnight.

8. Release the cheesecake from the pan when ready to serve and place on a plate. To decorate, whip the cream until stiff peaks form and then swoosh it over the top of the cheesecake like the foam on an espresso martini! Decorate with chocolate covered coffee beans and a dusting of cocoa powder.

FOR THE BASE

9oz (250g) pack speculoos cookies
5½ tbsp (80g) unsalted butter, melted

FOR THE CHEESECAKE

2 tbsp instant coffee granules
2 tbsp boiling water
1lb 5oz (600g) cream cheese
¼ cup (30g) all-purpose flour
1 cup (200g) light brown sugar
4 large eggs
⅔ cup (150ml) sour cream
4 tbsp coffee liqueur

TO DECORATE

scant 1 cup (200ml) whipping cream
chocolate covered coffee beans
1 tsp cocoa powder

8 in (20 cm) round springform pan, greased and base lined with parchment paper

MILLIONAIRE ÉCLAIRS

Makes 8

FOR THE SALTED CARAMEL PASTRY CREAM

½ batch Salted Caramel
  (see page 199), cooled
1 batch Thick Vanilla Pastry
  Cream (see page 196), cooled

FOR THE CHOUX PASTRY

3½ tbsp (50g) unsalted butter
½ cup (75g) white bread flour
¼ tsp salt
2 large eggs, beaten

FOR THE GANACHE

3½oz (100g) dark chocolate,
  chopped
scant 1 cup (200ml) whipping
  cream
1 tbsp light corn syrup
1¾ tbsp (25g) salted butter

TO DECORATE

2 graham crackers
gold leaf or edible gold dust

2 baking sheets, lined
2 large piping bags
large French star nozzle
nozzle of your choice

Make these and I guarantee you will feel like a millionaire.

1. Start by making the caramel and pastry cream the day before (or the morning before) you'd like the éclairs, as these need time to cool and éclairs are best served straight away with everything ready!

2. To make the choux, to a small saucepan add the butter and 6½ tablespoons (100ml) water and heat gently until the butter is melted. Bring to a boil and throw in all of the flour and salt. Beat well over a low heat for a couple of minutes more until the mixture is stiff and sticks well to itself.

3. Remove from the heat and beat for a minute to allow the mixture to cool. Add the eggs, a little at a time, while you continue to beat. You may not need all of the egg, but as soon as the mixture gets to dropping consistency (it drops off the spatula nicely), then the mix is ready. Leave to cool.

4. Preheat the oven to 400°F (200°C).

5. Put the cooled choux pastry into a large piping bag fitted with a large French star nozzle. Pipe eight éclairs about 5 in (12 cm) in length over the two parchment-lined baking sheets, leaving plenty of room between each one for them to puff up.

6. Bake for 20–25 minutes, or until dark golden brown.

7. Remove the éclairs from the oven and prick each one at the bottom a few times with a cocktail stick to allow the steam to escape. Leave to cool fully on a wire rack.

8. Combine the salted caramel and vanilla pastry cream in a large bowl. Whisk well for 2–3 minutes with a handheld electric whisk and then spoon into a piping bag with your favorite nozzle attached. Set aside.

9. For the ganache, add the chopped chocolate to a large bowl. Heat the cream to just below boiling in the microwave, about 1–2 minutes. Pour the cream over the chocolate and leave to stand for 2 minutes. Stir well to combine, then add the corn syrup and butter, and stir again. Transfer the ganache to a rectangular dish to make dipping the éclairs easier.

10. Slice the éclairs in half lengthwise. Pipe some salted caramel pastry cream onto the base of the éclairs in blobs or waves—baker's choice! Dip the top halves in the ganache and place on top of the bases carefully. Crumble over some graham crackers and brush on some gold leaf or spritz with gold dust!

LEMON & STRAWBERRY MERINGUE CAKE

Serves 10

This cake brings me summer, even on a rainy day. This is the kind of dessert that you want to take to a picnic—it's beautiful and packed with flavor.

FOR THE MERINGUE

6 large egg whites
1 tsp white wine vinegar or
  lemon juice
1¾ cups (360g) sugar
½ tsp pink gel food coloring
  (oil free)
1¾oz (50g) almonds, finely chopped

FOR THE STRAWBERRY COULIS

14oz (400g) strawberries, hulled
  and halved
juice of 1 lemon
1¼ cups (150g) powdered sugar,
  or to taste
1 tbsp vanilla paste

FOR THE LEMON CREAM

2½ cups (600ml) whipping cream
1 batch Lemon Curd
  (see page 199), cooled

FOR THE TOPPINGS

10½oz (300g) strawberries,
  hulled, some halved and some
  quartered
1¾oz (50g) almonds, roughly
  chopped

4 baking sheets, lined

1. Using an 8in (20cm) cake pan as a guide, draw an 8in (20cm) circle on four sheets of parchment paper and place pencil-side down on four baking sheets. Set aside.

2. Preheat the oven to 325°F (160°C).

3. In a stand mixer (cleaned with a little extra white wine vinegar or lemon juice), add the egg whites and white wine vinegar or lemon juice and start to whisk on medium speed for 5 minutes until frothy. Slowly increase the speed until you are on maximum and stiff peaks form. Turn the speed down to medium and slowly add the sugar, a spoonful at a time, and keep whisking until the meringue is super glossy and thick, about 5 minutes.

4. Remove one-third of the meringue and mix the pink food coloring into it. Add the pink meringue back into the bowl and carefully fold it through the white meringue to create a beautiful marble effect. Divide the mixture among the four circles and spread it to the edges. Sprinkle the almonds over the tops.

5. Bake for 45 minutes–1 hour until dry.

6. Turn the oven off and put a wooden spoon in the door to keep it open a crack. Leave them in the oven to cool completely.

7. While the meringues are cooling, make the strawberry coulis. Add the strawberries, lemon juice, powdered sugar, and vanilla paste to a saucepan and place over medium heat. Bring to a boil and let reduce down until thickened slightly and jammy, about 10–15 minutes. Taste for sweetness and, depending on the season, you may need to add slightly more sugar. Set aside to cool completely.

8. For the lemon cream, whip the cream to soft peaks and swirl the lemon curd through.

9. To assemble the meringue cake, start with a meringue on the bottom and add one-quarter of the lemon cream followed by one-quarter of the coulis. Repeat this process until you reach the final layer.

10. To finish, top with the fresh strawberries and chopped almonds for a final flourish.

KEY LIME PIE DEUX MILLE FEUILLE

Serves 6

FOR THE ROUGH PUFF PASTRY

2¾ cups (350g) all-purpose flour
1 tsp fine sea salt
1 cup plus 2 tbsp (250g) unsalted
  butter, frozen
10–14 tbsp ice-cold water

FOR THE PASTRY CREAM

1½ batches Thick Vanilla Pastry
  Cream (see page 196), cooled
finely grated zest and juice of
  2 limes

TO DECORATE

3 gingersnaps
lime zest spirals

baking sheet, lined
piping bag
round nozzle

Making rough puff pastry can be therapeutic, and for children, it can improve their motor skills—squeezing the butter and flour, rolling out the pastry, and folding it up again. It's a great bonding experience if you want to make this one with your kids. Lamination for the nation!

1. Start with the rough puff pastry. Sift the flour and salt into a large mixing bowl. Grate in the frozen unsalted butter using a coarse box grater and then gently toss the flour and butter together. Add the ice-cold water, a little at a time, and gently mix with a butter knife until a dough begins to form.

2. At this stage, squish the dough together with your hands, being careful not to handle it too much, until a rough dough ball forms. Don't squish the butter in too much; you want to see streaks of it in the dough. Flatten the dough into a rough rectangle, then wrap it in plastic wrap and chill in the fridge for 30 minutes or freezer for 15 minutes.

3. While the dough is chilling, you can make the pastry cream and leave that to cool in the fridge.

4. Once chilled, roll out the dough to a 8 x 12 in (20 x 30 cm) rectangle and fold it into thirds, like a letter. Wrap again and chill for another 15 minutes.

5. Repeat this rolling and folding process twice more, and the dough will begin to look smoother. On the final roll, make a 12 x 16 in (30 x 40 cm) rectangle, wrap in plastic wrap and leave to chill in the fridge for a further 30 minutes.

6. Preheat the oven to 350°F (180°C).

7. Place the pastry on the parchment-lined baking sheet, cover with another piece of parchment paper, and place two more baking sheets on top. Weigh them down with another heavy dish and bake for 35–40 minutes until golden brown. If the center isn't golden brown after this time, but the edges are, you can cover the edges with foil and bake for another 10–15 minutes uncovered to even out the color. Leave to cool.

8. Remove the pastry cream from the fridge and add the zest and juice from the limes. Use a handheld electric whisk to beat the cream until light and airy. Pop in a piping bag fitted with a round nozzle.

9. Carefully, using a bread knife, cut the pastry sheet into 18 small equal-size rectangles. Pipe dots of lime pastry cream onto six of the pastry rectangles and then cover with another piece of pastry. Repeat twice more. Decorate the final layer of pastry cream with crumbled gingersnaps and make some spirals of lime zest with a peeler, if you like!

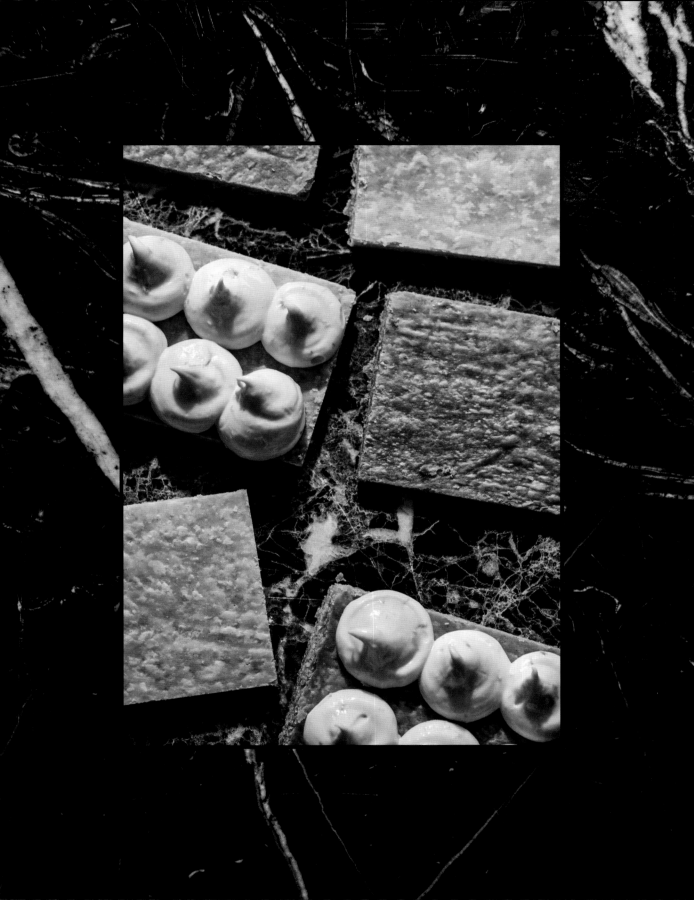

MADELEINE BABA

Serves 6–9

For this bake, the hero is the syrup. The madeleines are so cute and tasty, but when dipped in that wonderful boozy syrup, it gives that special kick that I think is always needed.

1. Start by melting the butter in the microwave. Use a pastry brush to brush the madeleine mold with some of the butter. Use a small sieve and dust the shells with flour to coat well, tapping out any excess. Set aside. Set the remaining butter aside to cool.

2. Using a handheld electric whisk, beat the eggs and sugar together until thick and airy. Add the orange zest and fold through. Sift in the flour, baking soda, and baking powder in two parts, folding through between each addition. Add the salt and then drizzle in the cooled melted butter, stirring to mix well. Rest in the fridge for a minimum of 30 minutes, or up to 6 hours.

3. Make the baba syrup by adding all the ingredients to a small saucepan and heating gently to dissolve the sugar.

4. When you're ready to bake the madeleines, preheat the oven to 400°F (200°C).

5. Add a heaped tablespoon of batter into each of the shells and bake for 10 minutes. Leave in the mold for 2 minutes before turning out onto a wire cooling rack. Re-grease and flour the mold, and then bake another half batch; you should get around 18 madeleines altogether.

6. Dip each madeleine in the syrup and serve with an extra drizzle! I like to serve 2–3 per portion in a small bowl.

FOR THE MADELEINES

½ cup plus 2 tbsp (140g) unsalted butter
2 large eggs
½ cup (100g) sugar
finely grated zest of 1 orange
1 scant cup (125g) all-purpose flour, plus extra for dusting
½ tsp baking soda
1½ tsp baking powder
⅛ tsp salt

FOR THE BABA SYRUP

1 cup (200g) sugar
5 tbsp (75ml) dark rum
juice of 1 orange (use the orange above and make up to ½ cup/ 120ml with water, if needed)

12-hole madeleine mold

LIFT YOUR
SPIRITS

This chapter is for those days when you're really not feeling yourself.

The ones where you look in the mirror, look away, and decide to stay tucked up in bed because it's just one of those days. I'm here for you. This is what this book is all about: baking with a vibe, even if the vibe isn't your happiest to start with. The recipes you find in this book are all made to give you a mood boost (if it's not through baking, then it might be through eating them). Either way, these comforting bakes, like Sticky Banana Cake (see page 64) or Emergency Pick-Me-Up Cookies (see page 70), can be taken back to bed for eating while watching a movie. Remember it's okay to have off days—you're only human after all.

THE ULTIMATE RED VELVET LAYERED CAKE

Serves 18–20

FOR THE CAKE

5½ cups (700g) all-purpose flour
¾ cup (75g) cocoa powder
6 tsp baking powder
3 tsp baking soda
3½ cups (700g) light brown sugar
2½ tsp salt
scant 2 cups (450ml) vegetable oil
2½ cups (600ml) buttermilk
3 tbsp vanilla paste
2 tbsp red gel or paste food
    coloring
6 large eggs

FOR THE CREAM CHEESE FROSTING

2 cups (450g) unsalted butter,
    softened
11½ cups (1.6kg) powdered sugar
1lb 5oz (600g) full-fat cream
    cheese
2 tbsp vanilla paste

*4 (8 in/20 cm) round cake pans,
greased and lined*

Who doesn't love a classic red velvet cake? I call this the ultimate because I have created layer upon layer of that red velvety cake and cream cheese filling. Give me a slice of this and it will definitely boost my mood.

1. Preheat the oven to 350°F (180°C).

2. In a large bowl, sift in the flour, cocoa powder, baking powder, and baking soda. Stir in the light brown sugar and salt, and make a well in the center.

3. In another large bowl, add the oil, buttermilk, vanilla, red food coloring, and eggs. Whisk together to combine.

4. Slowly pour the wet ingredients into the dry, whisking continuously in one direction only to avoid lumps. Whisk until you have a smooth batter and then divide it among the cake pans. (You can also bake in two batches—leave half the batter in the fridge while you bake the first two cakes.)

5. Bake for 35–40 minutes until well risen and a skewer inserted into the middle comes out clean. Leave to cool in the pans for 10 minutes and then turn out onto a wire rack to cool completely.

6. Make the cream cheese frosting by adding the butter to a stand mixer fitted with a paddle attachment. Sift in half the powdered sugar and then beat for 2–3 minutes. Sift in the remaining powdered sugar and then beat for a further 3–4 minutes until super pale and fluffy. Add the cream cheese and vanilla paste, and beat slowly until smooth. Don't over mix or it will loosen too much. Spoon into two large piping bags and leave in the fridge until you are ready to use.

7. When all four cakes have cooled, use a bread knife to level the domed tops and then carefully slice each cake horizontally into three, giving you 12 thin layers of cake. Save any trimmings for decoration.

8. Use a turntable to pipe equal amounts of frosting onto 11 of the layers, and then stack them on top of one another, being careful when moving them, because they are super delicate! Add the plain layer on top and pop the cake in the fridge for 30 minutes or the freezer for 15 minutes until firmed up.

9. Crumb-coat the cake and chill again until firm.

10. Finish the cake with a final layer of cream cheese frosting, smoothing it out to finish. Crumble up your cake trimmings and use to embellish the top how you like.

STICKY BANANA CAKE

Serves 9–12

LIFT YOUR SPIRITS

Banana and caramel is a combo I always say yes to, and this is a twist on a traditional Angolan recipe. Growing up, these were the flavors I loved, and I remember how much I loved waking up in the morning and smelling banana cake in the oven. It was just everything to me (thanks Mum).

1. Grease the bottom and sides of the cake pan, and line with two long strips of parchment paper crossing over one another on the base (so each side is covered). Preheat the oven to 325°F (160°C).

2. In a heavy-bottomed saucepan, add 1 cup (200g) of the sugar with a splash (approximately 1 tbsp) of water. Put the heat on low to let the sugar dissolve and then slowly increase the heat to a fierce bubble. Let color and caramelize until dark brown. Pour into the bottom of the cake pan and add the sliced bananas in a single layer.

3. To make the cake, whip the remaining ½ cup (100g) sugar with the margarine, light brown sugar, vanilla paste, and cinnamon until light and fluffy. Add the eggs, one at a time, with a spoonful of flour if the batter starts to split. Whip in the 2 mashed bananas.

4. Sift in the flour and baking powder and fold in gently. Pour the cake mixture into the lined pan over the sliced bananas and bake for 45 minutes–1 hour until golden brown and a skewer inserted into the middle comes out clean.

5. Leave to cool in the pan for 15–20 minutes and then turn out—don't let it cool completely in the pan or the caramel will set! Serve with a dollop of crème fraîche, if you like.

1½ cups (300g) sugar, divided
8 bananas, 6 sliced lengthwise
    and 2 mashed
1 cup plus 2 tbsp (250g)
    margarine
¾ cup (150g) light brown sugar
1 tsp vanilla paste
1 tsp ground cinnamon (optional)
4 large eggs
1¾ cup plus 2 tbsp (250g)
    all-purpose flour
2¼ tsp baking powder
1 tsp salt

TO SERVE (OPTIONAL)

crème fraîche

8 in (20 cm) square cake pan

RHUBARB & CUSTARD LAYER CAKE

Serves 10

FOR THE CAKE

2 cups (450g) margarine
2¼ cups (450g), plus 2 tbsp sugar, divided
8 large eggs
scant 3½ cups (450g) all-purpose flour
1 tsp salt
4 tsp baking powder
4 tbsp cornstarch
¼ tsp vanilla extract
6½ tbsp (100ml) milk

FOR THE BUTTERCREAM

2 cups (450g) unsalted butter, softened
7 cups (1kg) powdered sugar, sifted
2 tbsp cornstarch
1 tbsp sugar
⅛ tsp vanilla extract
3½ tbsp (50ml) milk

FOR THE RHUBARB SHARDS

1½ cups (300g) sugar
pink gel or paste food coloring
1 stick rhubarb

TO ASSEMBLE

1lb (450g) rhubarb jam
½ batch Vanilla Pastry Cream (see page 196), cooled

4 (8in/20cm) round cake pans, greased and lined
baking sheet, lined

Who doesn't love a rhubarb and custard boiled sweet, and by extension a rhubarb and custard bake? Honestly, my favorite part of this bake is the rhubarb shards, but the whole ensemble is just stunning.

1. Preheat the oven to 350°F (180°C).

2. Whip the margarine and 2¼ cups (450g) sugar until light, fluffy, and pale. Add the eggs, one at a time. If the mix seems to be splitting, add a spoonful of the flour to get it back on track. Add the flour, salt, and baking powder in a couple of batches and fold through gently.

3. Mix together the cornstarch, sugar, vanilla extract, and milk and then add this to the cake mix. Divide the batter among the cake pans (if baking in two batches, pop the second two in the fridge while the first two bake).

4. Bake for 25–30 minutes until golden on top and a skewer inserted into the center comes out clean. Leave in the pans to cool for 10 minutes and then turn out onto a wire cooling rack. Turn the oven down to 240°F (120°C).

5. Make the custard buttercream by whipping the butter until light and fluffy—almost pale white. Add the powdered sugar in spoonfuls and continue to beat for a few minutes. Make another custard mixture with the cornstarch, sugar, vanilla extract, and milk, and then beat this into the buttercream. Transfer the buttercream to a piping bag, snip off the tip, and set aside.

6. For the rhubarb shards, make a sugar syrup with the sugar, a dash of pink coloring (if it's outdoor rhubarb season), and 1¼ cups (300ml) water, and then peel strips of rhubarb into it. Let it bubble for about 3–4 minutes and then turn off the heat. Leave for 10 minutes and then transfer the rhubarb onto the lined baking sheet (reserving the syrup). Pop into the low oven for 30–35 minutes and then either leave on the tray to harden or twirl around wooden spoon handles/skewers to make curls.

7. Trim any domes off the cakes to level them out. Use a few tablespoons of the remaining rhubarb sugar syrup to drizzle over the cakes.

8. Pipe a circle of buttercream around the edge of three of the cakes. Fill in the middles with the rhubarb jam (reserving 1¾oz/50g jam) and then add dots of pastry cream over the jam. Stack the cake, finishing with the un-iced layer on top. Place in the fridge for 30 minutes.

9. Crumb-coat the cake with more buttercream and chill again, either in the fridge or freezer until very cold. Finish with another layer of buttercream and add a few swooshes of the reserved rhubarb jam around the cake, using a scraper to blend them in together and create a cool marble effect.

10. Add the rhubarb shards and twists over the top to finish off.

EMERGENCY PICK-ME-UP COOKIES

Makes 20

LIFT YOUR SPIRITS

This has to be the best pick-me-up recipe ever. Once you have got the dough together, you can literally add anything that makes you feel better, so whether it's your favorite nuts or favorite chocolate bar, this cookie is all about you. Pop them in the freezer, ready to be baked whenever you're in need of a pick-me-up!

1. Cream together the butter, sugar, and light brown sugar really well in a stand mixer fitted with a paddle attachment (or in a mixing bowl with a handheld electric whisk) for about 4–5 minutes. Add the egg and vanilla paste and beat until smooth.

2. Sift the flour, salt, baking soda, and baking powder into the bowl and continue to beat until dough crumbs begin to form, about 20–30 seconds.

3. At this stage add in your favorite chopped chocolate (or a mix) and then divide into 20 balls, about 3 tbsp each. Squidge them down slightly to make a puck shape, place on a baking sheet, and open-freeze for 8–12 hours. Once frozen, transfer to a freezer bag and store in the freezer for up to 3 months.

4. When you have a bad day, a good day, or just fancy a cookie, preheat the oven to 350°F (180°C), pop your chosen number of cookies on the lined baking sheet, sprinkle with sea salt, and bake for 14–16 minutes until golden around the edges.

5. Leave to cool on the sheet for 5 minutes and then devour and cheer yourself up!

½ cup plus 2 tbsp (150g)
    unsalted butter
½ cup (100g) sugar
½ cup (100g) light brown sugar
1 egg, beaten
1 tsp vanilla paste
2 cups (275g) all-purpose flour
1 tsp salt
½ tsp baking soda
½ tsp baking powder
10½oz (300g) dark/milk/white
    chocolate, roughly chopped
flaky sea salt

baking sheet, lined

CHURRO BITES

Makes 40-45

These are so easy to make and a good way to start making choux pastry. You can also pipe these into heart shapes on baking sheets and fry up some heart-y churros!

1. Start with the churro batter by heating the milk, butter, sugar, and salt with 6½ tablespoons (100ml) water in a small saucepan over medium heat. While heating, in a separate bowl beat together the eggs and vanilla paste, and set aside.

2. Once the milk mixture has begun to boil, add in all the flour and beat well until the mixture becomes thick. Take off the heat and continue beating for another minute to cool the mixture. Slowly add the egg mixture, a little at a time, while beating. Make sure the batter is smooth again before adding the next batch, it will separate before it becomes smooth, so don't panic. Leave the mix to cool while you heat the oil.

3. Heat the oil in a large saucepan to 375°F (190°C), or until a small piece of bread sizzles and floats when you add it. Add the churro batter to a piping bag fitted with a star nozzle.

4. Using a pair of scissors in one hand and the piping bag in the other, squeeze the churros in bite-size pieces, about 2 in (5 cm) long, into the oil, snipping off the batter carefully to add them to the pan.

5. Fry for 2–3 minutes until golden, then remove with a slotted spoon onto a paper-towel-lined plate. Continue to use all of the batter up.

6. In a large bowl mix the sugar and cinnamon together and add the churro bites, a handful at a time, tossing well to coat.

7. To make the chocolate sauce, add the chocolate to a small bowl and heat the cream in the microwave until just below boiling, about 1–2 minutes. Pour the cream over the chocolate and leave for 2 minutes. Add the salt and sugar, and whisk together until smooth.

8. Serve the chocolate sauce alongside the churro bites straight away.

FOR THE BATTER

⅔ cup (150ml) whole milk
3 tbsp (40g) unsalted butter
2 tbsp (25g) sugar
½ tsp fine sea salt
2 large eggs, beaten
1 tbsp vanilla paste
1⅓ cups (175g) all-purpose flour
about 4 cups (1 liter) vegetable oil, for frying

FOR THE CINNAMON SUGAR

¼ cup (50g) sugar
1 tbsp ground cinnamon

FOR THE CHOCOLATE SAUCE

3½oz (100g) dark chocolate, roughly chopped
scant 1 cup (200ml) whipping cream
1 tsp flaky sea salt
1 tsp sugar

piping bag
star nozzle

DARK CHOCOLATE & CARAMEL MOUSSE

Makes 6

FOR THE CARAMEL

1 batch Caramel (see page 199), cooled

FOR THE COOKIE BASE

7oz (200g) chocolate wafer cookies, crushed
5 tbsp (80g) unsalted butter, melted
1 tsp edible gold glitter

FOR THE CHOCOLATE MOUSSE

9oz (250g) dark chocolate, roughly chopped
3½ tbsp (50g) unsalted butter
6 large eggs, separated

TO DECORATE

⅔ cup () 150ml whipping cream
toffee popcorn
gold edible glitter

2 piping bags
6 dessert glasses
star nozzle

I am such a mousse fan, I love how it just melts and disappears in the mouth. Here, the mousse sits between a cookie base and some crunchy toffee popcorn. The only problem is one is never enough!

1. Start by making the caramel, letting it cool completely at room temperature, and popping into a piping bag. Knot the end so it doesn't escape, and set aside.

2. Bash the chocolate wafer cookies to a fine crumb in a bag with a rolling pin. Add to a bowl with the melted butter and edible glitter, and stir to combine. Divide equally among the glasses and press down with the back of a spoon or shot glass. Pop in the fridge to set while you make the mousse.

3. Melt the chocolate and butter in the microwave and mix well. Add the egg yolks and mix. If they seize, add a little hot water, a tablespoon at a time, and mix well to smooth out. Add the egg whites to a clean bowl and whisk well to make stiff peaks. Fold these through the chocolate mixture carefully until no white spots remain.

4. Divide half the mousse evenly among the cookie bases and then drizzle over some caramel. Add the rest of the mousse on top and then refrigerate for 4 hours to set.

5. Just before serving, whip the whipping cream to stiff peaks and pop in a piping bag fitted with a star nozzle. Pipe a tall swirl on top of the mousse, drizzle with some extra caramel (pop the caramel in the microwave for 20 seconds to melt a bit), top with toffee popcorn, and then spritz all over with the gold dust.

Tip: the caramel keeps for 2 months, so leave in the bag and use to jazz up any other desserts!

RUM-SPICED PINEAPPLE TARTS

Makes 12

Let's give you some island vibes with these tarts—this is the kind of bake that will make you feel like you're somewhere nice and warm! From the tangy flavor of the pineapple to the punchiness of the rum, this recipe is the perfect way to lift your spirits and bring the vacation vibes into your home.

1. Make the pastry by popping all the ingredients, except the water, into a food processor and pulse to make fine crumbs. Slowly add the water, a tablespoon at a time, until it comes together. Turn the pastry out onto the work surface and bring it together gently.

2. Roll out the pastry to about ¼ in (5 mm) thick (it might be easier to do this in two pieces). Cut out 12 circles just larger than your tart pans and then press the pastry into the pans, pricking the bases with a fork. Pop the unbaked tart shells in the fridge for an hour or two. This is a great time to make your vanilla pastry cream and leave in the fridge to cool.

3. Preheat the oven to 400°F (200°C).

4. Line the pastry cases with parchment paper and then add baking weights into each one. Bake for 10 minutes, and then remove the baking weights and bake for another 10–15 minutes until cooked through and golden brown. Remove from the pans carefully and let cool on a wire rack.

5. For the pineapple filling, add the dark rum, dark brown sugar, vanilla paste, and butter to a large saucepan. If using canned pineapple, you can add the juice from the cans, too! Bring to a gentle simmer over medium heat and let the sugar dissolve. Working in batches, poach the pineapple rings for 5–8 minutes until soft. Let them cool on a wire rack over a baking dish to catch any of the lovely pineapple syrup dripping off them. If the poaching liquid is looking a little dry, a splash of water to keep it above the pineapple will help. When all the pineapple is cooked, cut your rings into small dice and set aside in a bowl.

6. Scrape any remaining pineapple syrup back into the saucepan and reduce slightly to a thick syrup. Pour half over the pineapples and toss through to coat.

7. Grab the pastry cream from the fridge, add 3–4 tablespoons of the remaining pineapple syrup, and, using a handheld electric whisk, whip it up until it is lighter and smoother. Add to a piping bag and snip off the tip.

8. To assemble the tarts, pipe a layer of pastry cream into the bottom of each tart shell. Divide the pineapple filling between them and then top with more dots of pastry cream. Add little pieces of crystallized ginger, if you like, and brush over some gold leaf for sparkle.

FOR THE PASTRY

scant 3½ cups (450g) all-purpose flour
1 cup plus 2 tbsp (250g) unsalted butter, cold and cubed
2 tbsp sugar
2 large egg yolks
6–8 tbsp ice-cold water

FOR THE PASTRY CREAM

1 batch Vanilla Pastry Cream (see page 196), cooled

FOR THE PINEAPPLE FILLING

6½ tbsp (100ml) dark rum
½ cup (100g) dark brown sugar
1 tsp vanilla bean paste
1¾ tbsp (25g) unsalted butter
1 medium pineapple, peeled and cored and sliced into 8–10 rings (or 10 rings canned pineapple in fruit juice)

TO DECORATE

4 large pieces crystallized ginger, finely diced (optional)
gold leaf

12 tartlet pans, greased
piping bag

TOUCH
THE SKY

Now, you know I love making big, grand, showstopping cakes. My Signature Splatter Cake, anyone?

In this chapter you will be able to take your baking to a new level. I show you how to make showstopper cakes the easy way. Don't get me wrong, this chapter is a challenging one, but it's all possible and I know you can do it. After this chapter you're going to feel like such a pro-baker and it's all down to your courage—and don't forget it's all about enjoying yourself, too. Put some music on and get baking.

TROPICAL CAKE

Serves 10

FOR THE CAKE

7oz (200g) dried, shredded coconut
2 cups (450g) margarine
2¼ cups (450g) sugar
8 large eggs
3½ cups (450g) all-purpose flour
4½ tsp baking powder
1 tsp salt
scant 1 cup (200ml) coconut milk

FOR THE PINEAPPLE CURD

1 (15oz/425g) can pineapple chunks
½ cup plus 2 tbsp (125g) sugar
5 tbsp (70g) unsalted butter
3 large eggs

FOR THE TROPICAL CREAM

1¾ cups (400ml) whipping cream
grated zest and juice of 1 lime
½ mango, peeled and finely chopped
1 passion fruit

FOR THE BUTTERCREAM

2 cups (450g) unsalted butter,
  softened
8½ cups (1.2kg) powdered sugar
6½ tbsp (100ml) coconut milk
  or 3½oz (100g) coconut cream

TO DECORATE

banana chips, mango slices,
  passion fruit halves, toasted
  coconut flakes

*4 (8in/20cm) round deep cake
pans, greased and lined
piping bag*

For the first showstopper we're going to the Caribbean. If you live in the UK like me, and don't always have the time to go on holiday to a nice Caribbean island, then making a cake that can transport you there is the next best thing.

1. Preheat the oven to 350°F (180°C).

2. Toast the coconut in a dry pan until pale golden, then leave to cool. Whip the margarine and sugar until light, fluffy, and pale. Add the eggs, one at a time. If the mix seems to be splitting, add a spoonful of the flour to get it back on track. Add the flour, baking powder, and salt in a couple of batches and fold through gently. Stir in the coconut milk and toasted coconut.

3. Divide the batter among the pans and bake for 25–30 minutes until golden on top and a skewer inserted into the center comes out clean.

4. Turn the oven off. Add the coconut flakes for decoration to a baking sheet and leave in the warm oven for 5 minutes until golden brown.

5. Leave the cakes in the pans to cool for 10 minutes and then turn out onto a wire rack to cool completely.

6. For the pineapple curd, drain the juice from the chunks (but keep it!) and chop the chunks into smaller pieces. Add the pineapple juice, sugar, and butter to a large heatproof bowl and place it over a pan of simmering water. Let the butter melt and then add the eggs. Whisk occasionally while it heats gently and thickens; about 25–30 minutes.

7. Dry the pineapple chunks with paper towels and then stir them into the curd. Cover the surface with plastic wrap. Let cool to room temperature and then pop in the fridge until you're ready to decorate.

8. For the tropical cream, add the cream and lime zest and juice to a bowl and whisk to soft peaks. Add the mango pieces (and any juice on the chopping board) and the passion fruit pulp and juice. Whisk again to stiff peaks.

9. For the buttercream, add the butter to a stand mixer fitted with the paddle attachment (or use a mixing bowl and handheld electric whisk) and beat until pale and fluffy. Add the powdered sugar in two batches, sifting well, and beat for 5–8 minutes until fluffy. Add the coconut milk and whip again until pale white and smooth. Transfer to a piping bag and snip off the tip.

10. Level the cakes to make them even and pipe a circle of coconut buttercream around the edge of the first. Add one-third of the pineapple curd to the middle of the cake layer, followed by one-third of the tropical cream. Repeat this for the next two cakes, then finish with the final cake upside-down for the most level top.

11. Crumb-coat with more of the buttercream and chill for an hour to set really solid. Finish with an extra layer or two of buttercream and then use a palette knife horizontally to make soft ruffles or lines. Add the banana chips, mango slices, and passion fruit halves over the top and finish with the toasted coconut flakes.

ULTIMATE COOKIES & CREAM CAKE

Serves 10

FOR THE CAKE

2 cups (450g) margarine
2¼ cups (450g) sugar
2 tbsp vanilla paste
8 large eggs
3¼ cups (400g) all-purpose flour
1½ tsp salt
4 tsp baking powder
5oz (154g) chocolate sandwich
   cookies, broken
½ cup (50g) cocoa powder

FOR THE CREAM CHEESE FROSTING

½ cup plus 2 tbsp (140g) unsalted butter
7oz (210g) cream cheese
2½ cups (350g) powdered sugar

FOR THE BUTTERCREAM

2 cups plus 2 tbsp (500g) unsalted
   butter, softened
6½ cups (900g) powdered sugar
4oz (125g) chocolate sandwich
   cookies, crushed, plus extra
   (crushed and whole) to decorate
3½ tbsp (50ml) whole milk

FOR THE GANACHE DRIP

scant 1 cup (200ml) whipping cream
3½oz (100g) dark chocolate, roughly
   chopped

*4 (8in/20cm) round cake pans,
greased and lined
piping bag
nozzle of your choice*

Cookies and cream was the flavor combo of my first huge layered cake. I love to enjoy this cake with a tall glass of milk.

1. Preheat the oven to 350°F (180°C).

2. Whip the margarine, sugar, and vanilla paste until light, fluffy, and pale. Add the eggs, one at a time, and if the mix seems to be splitting, add a spoonful of the flour to get it back on track. Add the flour, salt, and baking powder in a couple of batches and fold through gently.

3. Split the cake batter between two bowls. Add the broken sandwich cookies into one half of the batter and fold in gently. Sift the cocoa powder into the other half of the batter and fold in gently.

4. Divide each batter between two cake pans and spread it to the edges. Bake for 20–25 minutes until risen and a skewer inserted into the middle of the cakes comes out clean. Leave to cool in the pans for 10 minutes before turning out onto a wire rack to cool completely.

5. While the cakes cool, make the cream cheese frosting. Beat together the ingredients for 3–4 minutes and set aside in the fridge.

6. For the buttercream, add the softened butter to a stand mixer fitted with the paddle attachment (or use a mixing bowl and handheld electric whisk) and beat until pale and fluffy. Add the powdered sugar in two batches, sifting in well, and then beat for 5–8 minutes until pale and fluffy. Add the crushed cookies and milk and beat to incorporate. Add the buttercream to a piping bag fitted with your favorite nozzle.

7. Once the cakes have cooled, trim the cakes to make them level (cut carefully as chunks of cookie might be in the way). To assemble, start with a golden cake and pipe a circle of buttercream around the edge. Fill the middle with one-third of the cream cheese frosting. Stack a chocolate cake on top and then repeat, following with another golden cake, and finally a chocolate. Chill for an hour.

8. Crumb-coat the cake in a thin layer of buttercream until smooth. Chill or freeze for 30 minutes. Finish with a final layer of buttercream, leaving around 6 tablespoons of icing in the piping bag for the final decor. Pop it in the fridge while you make the ganache drip.

9. Heat the cream in the microwave for 1–2 minutes until just below boiling. Pour over the chocolate and let sit for 2 minutes before stirring well to combine and make a smooth ganache.

10. Pour the ganache over the top of the cake and gently push toward the edges with the back of a spoon to help the ganache drip down the sides—use a teaspoon or cocktail stick to help edge it over.

11. Pipe six buttercream rosettes on the top of the cake and then finish with a final crumble of sandwich cookies and some extra whole ones.

I'LL BRING YOU FLOWERS

Serves 10

FOR THE CAKE

1½ cups (350g) unsalted butter, softened
1¾ cups (350g) sugar
grated zest and juice of 1 lemon
6 large eggs
2¾ cups (350g) all-purpose flour
¾ tsp salt
3½ tsp baking powder
1 tbsp rose water

FOR THE LEMON ROSE BUTTERCREAM

1½ cups plus 4 tbsp (375g) unsalted
  butter, softened
5⅓ cups (750g) powdered sugar, sifted
grated zest and juice of 1 lemon
1 tbsp rose water

FOR THE FLOWERS BUTTERCREAM

1 cup (250g) unsalted butter, softened
3½ cups (500g) powdered sugar, sifted
1 tbsp vanilla paste
1 tbsp whole milk
pink, green, yellow, and purple gel
  food coloring

TO DECORATE

sugar roses

*2 (8 in/20 cm) round cake pans,
greased and lined
4 piping bags
leaf, rose petal, open star, and 102
petal nozzles*

Why just bring flowers when you can bring flowers and cake?

1. Preheat the oven to 350°F (180°C).

2. Beat the butter, sugar, and lemon zest really well for 4–5 minutes until super light and fluffy. Scrape down the edges and add the eggs, a couple at a time, beating really well between each addition. If the mix seems to be splitting, add a spoonful of the flour to get it back on track. Sift in the flour, salt, and baking powder and fold in gently before adding the lemon juice and rose water.

3. Divide between the cake pans and bake for 25–30 minutes until well risen and a skewer inserted into the cakes comes out clean. Allow the cakes to cool in the pans for 10 minutes, then turn out onto a cooling rack to cool completely.

4. To make the lemon rose buttercream, add the softened butter to a stand mixer fitted with the paddle attachment (or use a mixing bowl and handheld electric whisk) and beat until pale and fluffy. Add the powdered sugar in two batches, sifting in well, and then beat for 5–8 minutes until pale and fluffy. Beat in the lemon zest and juice, and the rose water. Set aside.

5. To make the flowers buttercream, add the softened butter to a stand mixer fitted with the paddle attachment (or use a mixing bowl and handheld electric whisk) and beat until pale and fluffy. Add the powdered sugar in two batches, sifting in well, and then beat for 5–8 minutes until pale and fluffy. Beat in the vanilla paste and milk, then divide it among four bowls. Color them pink, green, yellow, and purple. Put each color buttercream into a piping bag fitted with an appropriate nozzle (put the green icing with the leaf nozzle, etc.).

6. Trim the domed tops off the cakes and then cut each one in half horizontally to give you four layers of cake.

7. Stack the four cake layers, adding an even layer of lemon rose buttercream between each layer. Crumb-coat the cake and place it in the fridge for 1 hour.

8. Finish the cake with a final smooth layer of lemon rose buttercream, or finish with a rustic flourish.

9. Decorate with sugar roses and then pipe on your favorite petal shapes and flowers all over the cake. Use the leaf tip to add green leaves to all of the flowers, including the sugar roses. Edible flowers also look gorgeous, if you can get your hands on them, between your sugared creations.

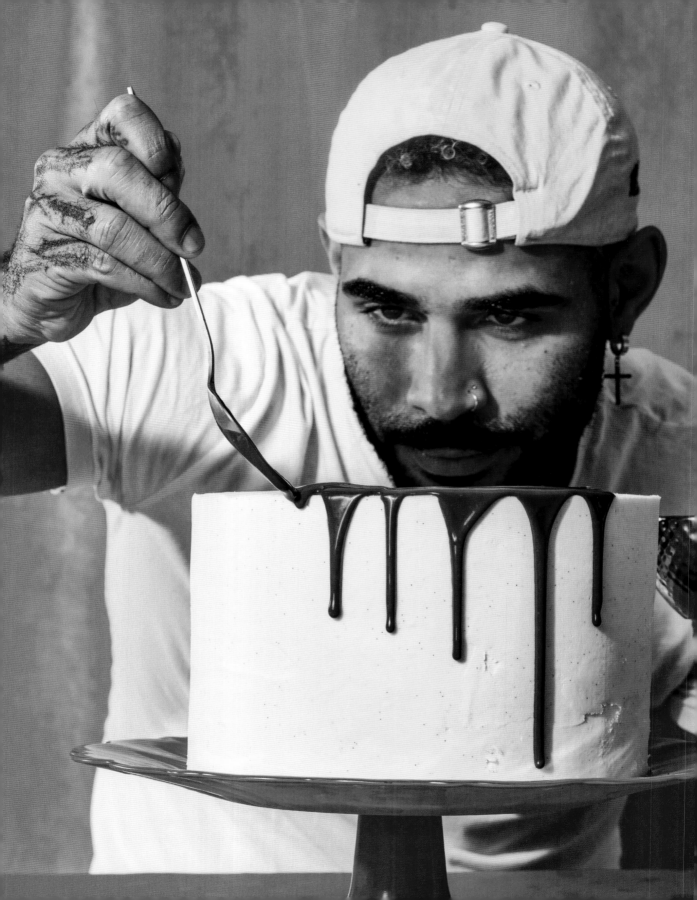

DRIP DRIP DRIP

Serves 14–16

Who doesn't love a drip cake? It always gives a dramatic finish—the cooler the cake, the cooler the drip.

FOR THE CHOCOLATE CAKE

3¾ cups (500g) all-purpose flour
1½ cups (150g) cocoa powder
2 tsp baking soda
2½ tsp baking powder
2 tsp fine sea salt
2 cups (400g) sugar
4 large eggs
1 cup (250ml) vegetable oil
2 cups (500ml) buttermilk
scant 2 cups (450ml) boiling water
2 tbsp vanilla paste

FOR THE BUTTERCREAM

1 batch Vanilla Buttercream
   (see page 196)

FOR THE GANACHE

5½oz (150g) milk chocolate, chopped
5½oz (150g) dark chocolate, chopped
1¼ cups (300ml) whipping cream
3 tbsp (40g) salted butter

FOR THE DRIP

1¾oz (50g) milk chocolate, chopped
1¾oz (50g) dark chocolate, chopped
scant 1 cup (200ml) whipping cream

TO DECORATE

¾oz (20g) milk chocolate
¾oz (20g) dark chocolate

*3 (8 in/20 cm) round cake pans,
greased and lined
piping bag
squeeze bottle (optional)*

1. Preheat the oven to 350°F (180°C).

2. In a large bowl sift together the flour, cocoa powder, baking soda, baking powder, and salt. Whisk in the sugar. Make a well in the center.

3. In a large mixing bowl, whisk together the eggs, oil, buttermilk, boiling water, and vanilla paste until smooth.

4. Whisking in one direction only (to prevent lumps), slowly pour the wet ingredients into the dry. When smooth, divide among the cake pans.

5. Bake for 25–30 minutes until risen and a skewer inserted into the cakes comes out clean. Let cool in the pans for 20 minutes before turning out onto a wire rack to cool completely.

6. Make the buttercream and pop it into a piping bag. You can refill it later if you need to.

7. For the ganache, add the milk chocolate and dark chocolate to a bowl and then heat the cream in the microwave until just below boiling, about 1–2 minutes. Pour the hot cream over the chocolate and leave for 2 minutes before stirring well to combine. Stir in the butter. Set aside.

8. Slice the domed tops off the cakes and then slice them in half so you have six layers (a turntable helps with even slicing).

9. Pipe a circle of buttercream around the edge of the first cake and fill the middle with around one-fifth of the ganache. Repeat this process until you finish with the final cake.

10. Crumb-coat the cake with more of the buttercream and then refrigerate for 1 hour or freeze for 30 minutes.

11. Using a cake scraper, ice the cake with most of the remaining buttercream until smooth and sharp, and then pop back in the fridge while you make your drips!

12. Make the drip in the same way as the ganache, but this time pop into a squeezy bottle or a piping bag with a small end cut off. Let cool to room temperature (but not set) and then carefully pipe drips all around the cake, using a cocktail stick to eek them down the sides if they need help. The cold cake will prevent them running all the way to the bottom.

13. Use any remaining buttercream for decorating the top, if you like, and then add chocolate shavings by using a peeler on the chocolate for decorating.

MY SIGNATURE SPLATTER CAKE

Serves 14

• TOUCH THE SKY

FOR THE CAKE

1 cup (100g) cocoa powder
1 tsp instant coffee granules
3½ tbsp (50ml) hot water
2¼ cups (450g) sugar
2 cups (450g) unsalted
  butter, softened
8 large eggs
scant 3½ cups (450g) all-purpose
  flour
3½ tsp baking powder
1 tsp fine sea salt

FOR THE BUTTERCREAM

1 batch Vanilla Buttercream
  (see page 196)

FOR THE SPLATTERS

7oz (200g) white chocolate,
  chopped
1¼ cups (300ml) whipping cream
5 different gel or paste food
  colorings

3 (8 in/20 cm) round cake pans,
greased and lined

I first made this cake 10 years ago and haven't changed a single thing! I absolutely love it.

1. Preheat the oven to 350°F (180°C).

2. Add the cocoa powder, instant coffee granules, and hot water to a small bowl and whisk to a smooth paste.

3. Beat the sugar and butter together until lighter in color, and then add the eggs, one at a time, beating well after each addition. Add the chocolate and coffee mix, and then sift in the flour, baking powder, and salt, and fold through.

4. Divide among the three pans and bake for 40–45 minutes, or until well risen and a skewer inserted into the center comes out clean. Leave to cool in the pans for 10 minutes before turning out onto a wire rack to cool completely.

5. When the cakes are cool, level them with a knife to make them easier to stack. Then, slice each cake in half horizontally to give you six layers in total.

6. Place the first layer, pipe buttercream on top, then place the remaining cakes, piping buttercream in between, putting the plain layer on top.

7. Crumb-coat the cake with more buttercream and refrigerate for 30 minutes or freeze for 15 minutes.

8. For the chocolate splatters, add the white chocolate to a bowl and heat the cream in the microwave for 1–2 minutes until just below boiling. Pour the hot cream over the chocolate and leave to stand for 2 minutes, then stir to a smooth ganache.

9. Divide the ganache among five bowls and color each a different color with food coloring (go as cute and pastel or as bold and vibrant as you like!), then let cool to room temperature.

10. Frost the cake with the remaining buttercream, giving it a smooth, sharp finish, and then refrigerate again until the buttercream hardens, around 20–30 minutes. This will give you a great canvas for your artistic splatters.

11. Now to have fun! Use a teaspoon to flick the colored ganache all over the cake (if it's a bit thick, you can blast it in the microwave at 10-second intervals to loosen it).

12. Let the ganache set for 15 minutes on the cake before serving.

PEANUT BUTTER & JELLY SHOWSTOPPER

Serves 12

FOR THE CAKE

1½ cups plus 4 tbsp (400g)
   unsalted butter, softened
4oz (120g) smooth peanut butter
2 cups (400g) sugar
6 large eggs
9oz (250g) plain yogurt
3¼ cups (400g) all-purpose flour
3 tsp baking powder
1½ tsp baking soda
1 tsp salt
1 cup (100g) ground almonds

FOR THE RASPBERRY JAM

1lb 2oz (500g) raspberries
1lb 2oz (500g) sugar
juice of 1 lemon
3 tsp fruit pectin powder

FOR THE PEANUT BUTTER BUTTERCREAM

1½ cups (350g) unsalted
   butter, softened
5½oz (150g) smooth 1 peanut butter
7 cups (1kg) powdered sugar

TO DECORATE

9oz (250g) peanuts, roasted
   and crushed

*2 (8 in/20 cm) round cake pans,
greased and lined
piping bag*

I've always loved mixing sweet flavors with savory flavors, and this is an all-American classic! People seem to either love or hate this combination, but I happen to LOVE it.

1. Preheat the oven to 350°F (180°C).

2. Beat together the butter, peanut butter, and sugar until pale and fluffy. Add the eggs, one at a time, beating well after each one. Add the yogurt and beat again briefly until combined.

3. Sift in the flour, baking powder, baking soda, and salt, and then fold these in gently with the ground almonds.

4. Divide the batter between the prepared cake pans and bake for 30–35 minutes until risen, and a skewer inserted into the middle comes out clean. Allow to cool in the pans for 10 minutes before turning out onto a wire rack to cool completely.

5. While the cakes are baking, make the raspberry jam filling. Pop the raspberries, sugar, and lemon juice in a heavy-bottomed saucepan over medium heat. Cook until the raspberries have softened and broken down, then bring the mixture to a boil for 5–8 minutes, carefully stirring. Take the jam off the heat, add the pectin powder, and bring to a boil, stirring, for one minute. Remove from the heat and allow to cool to room temperature, before placing in the fridge until ready to use.

6. For the peanut butter buttercream, add the softened butter and peanut butter to a stand mixer fitted with the paddle attachment (or use a mixing bowl and handheld electric whisk) and beat until pale and fluffy. Add the powdered sugar in two batches, sifting in well, and then beat for 5–8 minutes until smooth and much lighter in color. Transfer to a piping bag and snip off the tip.

7. Level the cakes with a serrated knife to make them easier to stack. Slice each cake horizontally in half to give you four layers of cake. Pipe a circle of buttercream around three of the cake layers and fill the circles with the raspberry jam (leaving some for the top, too).

8. Stack the cakes, putting the plain layer on top. Crumb-coat the cake with more buttercream and freeze for 10–15 minutes or refrigerate for 30 minutes.

9. Once the crumb coat is cold, frost the cake with the rest of the buttercream, making a slight border on the top to catch the jam. Add the remaining jam to the top of the cake and then use your hands to carefully stick the crushed peanuts around the bottom.

BURNED HONEY CAKE

Serves 8

FOR THE BURNED HONEY

12oz (350g) honey

FOR THE CAKE

1 cup (250g) unsalted butter, cut
   into cubes
4 large eggs
2½ cups (325g) all-purpose flour
2 tsp baking soda
¾ tsp salt
½ tsp cinnamon
3 tsp baking powder

FOR THE BURNED HONEY FROSTING

2 cups (250g) powdered sugar,
   sifted
½ cup plus 2 tbsp (150g) unsalted
   butter, softened

*8 in (20 cm) round cake pan,
greased and lined*

This cake is so delicate! It is so simple with only one hero ingredient, yet it goes such a long way. It is rich, yet light.

1. Preheat the oven to 325°F (160°C).

2. Add the honey to a large heavy-bottomed saucepan and heat over medium heat. Increase the heat, swirling from time to time until a slightly burned smell comes from the honey and it turns darker brown, about 3–5 minutes.

3. Measure out ⅓ cup (125g) of the burned honey in a heatproof bowl. Set aside.

4. For the cake, add the butter to the rest of the honey in the pan and stir to melt (you may need to heat it on low to help it along, if the butter is really cold). Leave to cool for 10 minutes.

5. When cool, whisk in the eggs, one at a time, and then sift in the flour, baking soda, salt, cinnamon, and baking powder. Mix to a smooth batter. It might be easier to whisk with a handheld electric whisk to speed this up.

6. Pour into the prepared cake pan and place on a baking sheet. Bake for 55–65 minutes until well risen and a skewer inserted into the center comes out clean. Check the cake after 45 minutes and cover with foil so the top doesn't brown too much. Leave to cool in the pan for 10 minutes before tipping out onto a wire rack to cool.

7. Make the frosting while the cake bakes so the honey doesn't cool too much and set hard. Add most of the reserved burned honey to a stand mixer (save a couple of tablespoons for drizzling) and beat well with half of the powdered sugar. Add the butter, a small piece at a time, scraping down well as the honey cools and sticks to the inside of the bowl. Beat well until smooth and then add the rest of the powdered sugar. Beat for another couple of minutes until smooth and set aside at room temperature until the cake is completely cool.

8. Swoosh the frosting over the top of the cake with a palette knife and then drizzle on the reserved burned honey.

OPERA CAKE

Serves 8

FOR THE JOCONDE SPONGE

6 large egg whites (4oz/120g if
  just buying whites)
3¼ tbsp (40g) sugar
2 cups (200g) ground almonds
1⅔ cups (200g) powdered sugar
6 large eggs
3 tbsp (25g) all-purpose flour
1¾ tbsp (25g) unsalted butter,
  melted

FOR THE COFFEE SYRUP

1 tbsp instant coffee granules
3½ tbsp (50ml) boiling water
1 tbsp sugar

FOR THE GANACHE

⅔ cup (150ml) whipping cream
3½oz (100g) dark chocolate,
  roughly chopped

FOR THE BUTTERCREAM

1 cup (250g) unsalted
  butter, softened
3½ cups (500g) powdered sugar
2 tsp instant coffee granules
2 tbsp boiling water

TO ASSEMBLE

½ batch Thick Vanilla Pastry
  Cream (see page 196), cooled
gold dust

*3 (8 in/20 cm) round cake pans,
greased and lined
piping bag*

Cut into this cake and hear the orchestra playing.

1. Preheat the oven to 400°F (200°C).

2. Start with the joconde sponge. In a stand mixer fitted with the whisk attachment (or use a mixing bowl and handheld electric whisk), whisk the egg whites to stiff peaks. Add the sugar, a spoonful at a time, whisking until glossy. Scrape into another bowl and set aside.

3. Add the almonds to the mixer bowl and sift in the powdered sugar. Add the whole eggs and whisk until thick and fluffy. Sift in the flour and fold in, and then add the melted butter. Fold the egg whites into the almond mixture and then divide among the three cake pans.

4. Bake for 8–10 minutes until golden brown and springy to the touch. Leave in the pans for 10 minutes and then tip out onto a wire cooling rack to cool completely.

5. While they cool, make the coffee syrup. Mix together the ingredients in a small bowl and then brush over the cooled cakes.

6. For the ganache, heat the cream in the microwave until just below boiling. Put the chocolate in a bowl, pour the hot cream over, and leave for 2 minutes. Stir together until smooth.

7. To make the buttercream, add the softened butter to a stand mixer fitted with the paddle attachment (or use a mixing bowl and handheld electric whisk) and beat until pale and fluffy. Add the powdered sugar in two batches, sifting in well, and then beat for 5–8 minutes until smooth and pale. Make the coffee mixture by stirring together the instant coffee and boiling water and then leaving for a couple of minutes. Add to the buttercream and whip again to mix through. Pop the buttercream into a piping bag and snip off the tip.

8. Now all the layers are ready we can assemble! Start with an almond sponge on the bottom and pipe a circle of coffee buttercream around the edge. Add the thick pastry cream in the middle and then top with another layer of sponge. Add another circle of buttercream and then fill this one with half of the ganache. Pop the final sponge on top.

9. Crumb-coat with more of the buttercream and refrigerate for a couple of hours.

10. Finish with the final layer of buttercream, smoothing round the cake. Put the remaining ganache in the microwave for 30 seconds to melt down again and then leave to cool to room temperature. Add to the top of the cake and let set before serving.

11. Finish with a spritz of gold dust for glam!

SEX ON THE BEACH CAKE

Serves 12

FOR THE CAKE

2 cups (450g) unsalted butter, softened
2¼ cups (450g) sugar
grated zest and juice of 1 orange
8 large eggs
3½ cups (450g) all-purpose flour
1½ tsp baking soda
3½ tsp baking powder
1 tsp salt

FOR THE COMPOTE

1 (15oz/420g) can peaches in syrup
2 large eggs, plus 2 large egg yolks
¾ cup (150g) sugar
6½ tbsp (100g) unsalted butter,
  cold and cubed
3½ tbsp (50ml) vodka

FOR THE SCHNAPPS CREAM

2 tbsp (30ml) cranberry juice
2 tbsp (30ml) peach schnapps
2½ tbsp (30g) sugar
1¼ cups (300ml) whipping cream

FOR THE BUTTERCREAM

2 cups (450g) unsalted butter, softened
7 cups (1kg) powdered sugar, sifted,
  plus up to 1 cup (150g) more
3½ tbsp (50ml) peach schnapps
5½oz (150g) canned peaches, pureed

TO DECORATE

fresh or canned peach slices

*4 (8 in/20 cm) round cake pans,
greased and lined
piping bag*

Now, this is more of an adult-themed summer tropical cake. It's one of those cakes you want to make when you just can't get out on holiday and need to feel an island vibe. Of course it has booze in it, too.

1. Preheat the oven to 350°F (180°C).

2. For the cake, beat the butter, sugar, and orange zest really well for 4–5 minutes until super light and fluffy. Scrape down the edges and add the eggs, a couple at a time, beating well between each addition. If the mix seems to be splitting, add a spoonful of the flour to get it back on track. Sift in the flour, baking soda, baking powder, and salt and fold gently through, then add the orange juice.

3. Divide among the pans and bake for 25–30 minutes until risen and a skewer inserted into the cakes comes out clean. Let cool in the pans for 10 minutes, then turn out onto a wire cooling rack to cool completely.

4. For the vodka peach compote, puree the canned peaches with their syrup, then add to a medium saucepan over low heat. Beat the eggs and yolks, then add to the pan with the sugar, and whisk well to combine. Heat gently until the sugar has dissolved. Increase the heat slightly and start to add the butter, a couple of cubes at a time. Stir constantly until thickened. Remove from the heat, add the vodka and then leave to cool in a container with a lid in the fridge.

5. For the cranberry schnapps cream, add the cranberry juice, schnapps, and sugar to a bowl and whisk to dissolve the sugar. Add the whipping cream and whip to stiff peaks.

6. To make the buttercream, add the softened butter to a stand mixer fitted with the paddle attachment (or use a mixing bowl and handheld electric whisk) and beat until pale and fluffy. Add the powdered sugar in two batches, sifting in well, and then beat for 5–8 minutes until smooth and pale. Add the schnapps and the peach puree and beat again to incorporate. If, after adding the puree, the buttercream seems to have split, add up to 1 cup (150g) more powdered sugar to bring it back together. Pop into a piping bag and snip off the tip.

7. Level the cakes to make them easier to stack. Pipe a circle of buttercream around three of the cakes. Fill each with one-third of the peach compote and cranberry schnapps cream. Stack the cakes, putting the plain one on top.

8. Crumb-coat with more buttercream and refrigerate for an hour or two until really firm.

9. Use the remaining buttercream to coat the cake with a crisp, sharp finish (or use a piping nozzle for rosettes around the top, if you like). Add extra peaches on the top to decorate and serve with a shot of schnapps on the side!

PROSECCO & RASPBERRY LAYERED CAKE

Serves 10

FOR THE CAKE

2 cups (450g) unsalted butter, softened
2¼ cups (450g) sugar
2 tbsp vanilla paste
8 large eggs
scant 3½ cups (450g) all-purpose flour
4 tsp baking powder
1 tsp salt
splash of prosecco

FOR THE PROSECCO-INFUSED RASPBERRY JAM

1lb 2oz (500g) raspberries
1lb 5oz (600g) sugar
scant 1 cup (200ml) prosecco
4 tsp fruit pectin powder

TO ASSEMBLE

1 batch Swiss Meringue Buttercream (see page 196)
pink gel or paste food coloring
6½ tbsp (100ml) prosecco
3½oz (100g) raspberries

3 (8in/20cm) cake pans, greased and lined
3 piping bags
star nozzle

This has to be one of my favorite-ever creations. I love this cake and it's perfect for any occasion, especially for a summer party or get-together. You can actually taste the prosecco!

1. Preheat the oven to 350°F (180°C).

2. Beat the butter, sugar, and vanilla paste really well for 4–5 minutes until super light and fluffy. Scrape down the edges and add the eggs, a couple at a time, beating really well between each addition. If the mix seems to be splitting, add a spoonful of the flour to get it back on track. Sift in the flour, baking powder, and salt, and fold gently through. Add a splash of prosecco to loosen slightly to dropping consistency.

3. Divide among the pans and bake for 30–35 minutes until well risen and a skewer inserted into the center comes out clean. Allow the cakes to cool in the pans for 10 minutes, and then turn out onto a wire cooling rack to cool completely.

4. While the cakes are cooling, make the raspberry jam by adding the raspberries, sugar, and prosecco to a small saucepan and heating gently over a low heat until the sugar has dissolved. Cook until the raspberries have softened and broken down, then bring the mixture to a boil for 5–8 minutes, carefully stirring. Take the jam off the heat, add the pectin powder, and bring to a boil, stirring, for one minute. Remove from the heat and allow to cool to room temperature, then pop in the fridge until ready to use.

5. Put one-third of the buttercream into a bowl and color it pink (I love a vibrant hot pink!), then add it to a piping bag and snip off the tip. Add the remaining two-thirds of the buttercream to a second piping bag and snip off the tip.

6. When the cakes are cool, slice off the domed tops to make for easy stacking. Slice each cake in half horizontally so you have six cakes in total. Brush each one with some prosecco.

7. Pipe a circle of the white buttercream around five of the cakes. Set aside 2½oz (75g) of the jam and then use the rest to fill the centers of the cakes.

8. Stack the cakes, finishing with the plain layer on top. Pop in the fridge for 15 minutes or in the freezer for 10 minutes.

9. Crumb-coat the cake with more white buttercream and chill again in the fridge for 30 minutes or in the freezer for 15 minutes.

10. When it comes to the final layer of buttercream, use the white and pink to create an ombre effect, a watercolor effect with swooshes, or your own design! Add a star nozzle and pipe rosettes on top.

11. Add the reserved jam to a piping bag and snip off the tip. Fill the raspberries with the jam, and use these to decorate your rosettes!

PECAN DANISH CAKE

Serves 12

FOR THE CAKE

1½ cups (350g) unsalted butter
1¾ cups (350g) sugar
1 tsp vanilla bean paste
6 large eggs
2¾ cups (350g) all-purpose flour
2 tsp baking powder
1 tsp ground cinnamon
½ tsp ground allspice
½ tsp ground nutmeg
5½oz (150g) chopped pecans

FOR THE FILLING

10½oz (300g) pecans
¾ cup (150g) light brown sugar
6 tbsp maple syrup
5 tbsp (75g) unsalted butter

FOR THE FROSTING

1 cup (225g) unsalted butter,
   softened
4½ cups (600g) powdered sugar
10½oz (300g) full-fat cream cheese
pinch salt
4 tbsp maple syrup

TO ASSEMBLE

1 batch Thick Vanilla Pastry
   Cream (see page 196), cooled
½ old croissant or Danish pastry

*2 (8 in/20 cm) round cake pans,
greased and lined
piping bag*

One of my favorite pastries is a pecan Danish. Honestly, if you want to make me happy, just turn up at my door with these pastries ... or with this cake.

1. Make the pastry cream and allow to cool completely. Pop it in the fridge. Preheat the oven to 350°F (180°C).

2. For the cake, beat the butter, sugar, and vanilla paste together until light and fluffy. Add the eggs, two at a time, beating well after each one. Add a spoonful of the flour if it looks like it's curdling. Sift in the flour, baking powder, cinnamon, allspice, and nutmeg, and fold through. Mix in the chopped pecans.

3. Divide the batter between the prepared pans and bake for 30–35 minutes until caramelized on top, well risen, and a skewer inserted into the center comes out clean. Allow to cool in the pans for 10 minutes before tipping out onto a wire cooling rack to cool completely.

4. To make the pecan and maple filling, roughly blitz the pecans in a food processor, then place in a saucepan with the light brown sugar, maple syrup, and butter. Cook over medium heat until the syrup begins to bubble, stirring occasionally. Allow to boil for 1 minute, then remove from the heat. Transfer the filling to a tray or plate, spread it out, and allow it to cool completely.

5. For the cream cheese frosting, in a stand mixer fitted with a paddle attachment (or using a mixing bowl and handheld electric whisk), beat the butter for 3 minutes on high. Sift in the powdered sugar and beat until pale and fluffy, about 4–5 minutes. Add the cream cheese, pinch of salt, and maple syrup and beat for another couple of minutes, no longer. Add to a large piping bag and snip off the tip.

6. Remove the pastry cream from the fridge and whip up with a handheld electric whisk until light and fluffy.

7. To assemble the cakes, level them with a serrated knife to make them easier to stack. Slice each cake horizontally in half to give you four layers of sponge. Pipe a circle of buttercream around three of the cake layers and fill the circles with a layer of pastry cream followed by one-quarter of the pecan and maple crumble on top. Stack the cakes, putting the plain layer on top.

8. Crumb-coat the cake with more buttercream and pop it in the fridge for an hour or the freezer for 30 minutes.

9. Frost the cake with the remaining buttercream, making it as smooth or as textured as you wish. Crumble the final quarter of the pecan and maple filling onto the top in the center, and then flake any leftover pastry from a croissant around the edge for a final flourish, if you like.

EASY-PEASY "I DO" WEDDING CAKE

Serves 20

FOR THE CAKE

4 cups (900g) margarine or
  unsalted butter
4½ cups (900g) sugar
4 tbsp vanilla paste
16 large eggs
7 cups (900g) all-purpose flour
6½ tsp baking powder
2 tsp salt

TO FILL AND DECORATE

2 batches Vanilla Buttercream
  (see page 196)
1 (14oz/400g) jar raspberry jam
gold leaf
fresh flowers

*2 (8 in/20 cm) round cake pans,
greased and lined
2 (6 in/15 cm) round cake pans,
greased and lined
2 (4 in/10 cm) round cake pans,
greased and lined
2 large piping bags
wooden dowels or jumbo straws*

Not everyone can afford a wedding cake, so I've made one that's easy-peasy. I do, do you?

1. Preheat the oven to 350°F (180°C).

2. Unless you've got two mixers, split the ingredients in half so you don't over mix or spill out the top.

3. Cream the butter, sugar, and vanilla paste until light and fluffy. Add the eggs, two at a time, until all the eggs are well incorporated. If the mix seems to be splitting, add a spoonful of the flour to get it back on track. Sift in the flour, baking powder, and salt in a couple of batches and fold through gently.

4. Divide the batter among the prepared pans so they're at the same level (obviously the larger pan will need more batter!) and then top them all up with the second batch of batter when you have made it.

5. If you can only bake a couple of cakes at a time, keep the filled pans in the fridge. Bake the cakes for 20–25 minutes until they have risen and are coming away from the sides of the pan. A skewer inserted into the middle should come out clean.

6. Leave the cakes to cool in their pans for 10 minutes before turning them out onto a wire cooling rack to cool completely. When cool, cut the domed tops off to make them easier to stack, and cut each one horizontally to give you four cakes of each size.

7. Make the buttercream and then pop it into two large piping bags and snip off the tips—no nozzles needed here! Pipe a spiral of buttercream over three of the cakes of each size, and spread evenly across them with a spatula. Add a circle of buttercream around the edge of each iced cake and fill the middles with jam.

8. Sandwich the cakes together according to size, topping each set with the plain cake layer. Add wooden dowels or jumbo straws into the 8 in (20 cm) and 6 in (15 cm) cakes; stick four in evenly to support the weight of the cakes.

9. Crumb-coat each cake with the buttercream and then refrigerate for an hour or until hard. (You can also freeze to speed this up!)

10. Stack the cakes on the final serving platter or plate. Finish the cakes with the remaining buttercream in your favorite style—you can cover it completely and crisply or leave in a semi-naked way. Use a paintbrush to carefully attach gold leaf over and add any fresh flowers you like (but remember, if they're not edible, make sure to remove them before serving).

IT'S A
FIESTA

I always think it's a fiesta, but even when it might not be, taking a bake with you will make it one!

I never go anywhere empty handed, and always try to take a fresh bake to any party or gathering. It does make me really popular at parties! If you're a bit shy or an introvert like me, then taking a bake to a fiesta is the perfect way to break the ice with people. You don't actually have to do anything apart from smile and wave—you've got the bake and that's all you need! This chapter is full of recipes that you can't just keep to yourself and you'll want to show off. Well, why not? Speculoos Cheesecake (see page 118), anyone?

ORANGE CRÈME BRÛLÉE CUPCAKES

Makes 12

FOR THE CUPCAKES

½ cup plus 4 tbsp (175g) unsalted
  butter, softened
¾ cup plus 2 tbsp (175g) sugar
grated zest and juice of 1 orange
3 large eggs
1⅓ cups (175g) all-purpose flour
1 tsp baking powder
½ tsp baking soda
½ tsp salt

TO DECORATE

1 cup (200g) sugar
1 batch Thick Vanilla Pastry
  Cream (see page 196), cooled
grated zest of 1 orange (optional)

*12-hole cupcake pan, lined
with paper cases
baking sheet, lined with a
silicone mat
piping bag
large round nozzle*

I'm actually obsessed with these cupcakes. The orange flavor coming from the cake paired with the custard frosting and caramelized top is everything.

1. Preheat the oven to 350°F (180°C).

2. Beat together the butter, sugar, and orange zest until super light and fluffy, about 4–5 minutes.

3. Beat in the eggs, one at a time, and then fold in the flour, baking powder, baking soda, and salt in two halves. Squeeze in half the orange juice (save the other half for the brûlée shards) and then divide the mixture among the 12 cupcake cases.

4. Bake for 20–23 minutes until golden and a skewer inserted into the middle comes out clean.

5. To make the brûlée shards for the decoration, add the sugar to a small skillet or saucepan and squeeze in the remaining orange juice. Swirl around over low heat until the sugar has dissolved and then turn the heat up to medium and let the caramel bubble until it's turned a darker golden color. Keep going until you can smell a near-to-burned sugar smell and then pour out immediately onto the silicone-lined baking sheet. Remember: brûlée means burned, so you do want a slightly smoky flavor here! Leave to harden for 15 minutes and then snap into 12 shards.

6. Whip up the pastry cream, adding the orange zest if using, and pop into a piping bag with a large round nozzle.

7. Pipe a circle of pastry cream onto each cupcake and then stick a brûlée shard in each one just before serving.

EASY PORTUGUESE CUSTARD TARTS

Makes 12

This is my take on the best Portuguese tart that I have ever had, which was eaten on holiday once in Porto. Delicious. This recipe isn't too tricky, so do give it a go!

1. Place the egg yolks, sugar, and cornstarch into a saucepan and whisk until smooth. Add the whole milk and stir to combine. Place over medium heat and stir continuously until the mixture thickens, and then boil for 1 minute.

2. Remove from the heat and add the vanilla paste. Scrape into a bowl, cover the surface with plastic wrap to prevent a skin forming, and then leave to cool completely at room temperature.

3. Preheat the oven to 400°F (200°C) and remove the pastry from the fridge (it needs about 15 minutes at room temperature before you use it).

4. Unroll the pastry, cut out 12 circles, and add to the greased muffin pan. Spoon in the cooled custard and level the top.

5. Bake for 25–30 minutes, or until golden and a little charred on top. Leave to cool in the pan for 30 minutes, and then tip out onto a wire cooling rack to cool completely.

6. Serve with a pinch of cinnamon over the top if you like.

Tip: You can re-roll any spare pastry afterward for easy jam tarts: just line a cupcake pan with pastry circles, add a teaspoon of jam and bake for about 15 minutes at 400°F (200°C).

2 large egg yolks
½ cup plus 2 tbsp (125g) sugar
2 tbsp cornstarch
1¾ cups (400ml) whole milk
2 tsp vanilla paste
2 (12½oz/360g) sheets ready-
  rolled puff pastry
½ tsp cinnamon (optional)

12-hole muffin pan, greased
4in (10cm) round cutter

STICKY CARAMEL CELEBRATION CAKE

Serves 10

FOR THE CAKE

2 cups (450g) unsalted butter, softened
1 cup (200g) sugar
1 cup (200g) light brown sugar
1¼oz (40g) blackstrap molasses
1 tsp vanilla bean paste
8 large eggs
3½ cups (450g) all-purpose flour
2 tsp baking powder
1 tsp baking soda

FOR THE TOFFEE SAUCE

6½ tbsp (100ml) whipping cream, plus extra if needed
½ cup (100g) dark brown sugar
1¼oz (40g) blackstrap molasses
6½ tbsp (100g) unsalted butter

TO ASSEMBLE

1 batch Swiss Meringue Buttercream (see page 196)

TO DECORATE

3½–5½oz (100–150g) caramel popcorn

2 (8 in/20 cm) round cake pans, greased and lined
piping bag

I'm sure you guys can tell by now, I love caramel! A sticky caramel cake will stay stored in my fridge until I'm done.

1. Preheat the oven to 350°F (180°C).

2. Beat the butter, sugar, light brown sugar, molasses, and vanilla paste for 4–5 minutes until super light and fluffy. Scrape down the edges and add the eggs, a couple at a time, beating well between each addition. If the mix seems to be splitting, add a spoonful of the flour to get it back on track.

3. Sift in the flour, baking powder, and baking soda, and fold gently through. Divide between the pans and bake for 40–45 minutes until well risen and a skewer inserted into the middle comes out clean. Allow the cakes to cool in the pans for 10 minutes, then turn out onto a wire cooling rack and leave to cool completely.

4. While the cakes are baking, make the toffee sauce. Pop the whipping cream, dark brown sugar, and molasses in a saucepan over medium heat, and cook until the sugar has dissolved, swirling the pan a few times. Once the sugar has dissolved, increase the heat to high and allow the sauce to bubble for about 3 minutes, stirring often to avoid the sauce burning. Remove from the heat, add the butter, and stir until well combined. If it's too tacky and doesn't seem like it will spread onto the cake layers easily, add a splash more whipping cream and return to the heat for a minute. Leave to cool to room temperature.

5. To assemble the cakes, level them with a serrated knife to make them easier to stack. Slice each cake in half horizontally to give you four layers.

6. Put the Swiss meringue buttercream in a piping bag and snip off the tip.

7. Pipe a circle of buttercream around three of the cake layers and fill the circles with one-quarter of the toffee sauce. Stack the cakes, putting the plain layer on top.

8. Crumb-coat the cake with more of the buttercream and pop it in the fridge for 1 hour or the freezer for 30 minutes.

9. When the crumb coat is totally cold, frost the cake with the remaining buttercream, making it smooth and sharp with a cake scraper. Refrigerate again for 20 minutes.

10. If the remaining toffee sauce has cooled and hardened, pop it in the microwave for 10–20 seconds or mix in 1 tablespoon boiling water to loosen it again. Spoon the toffee sauce onto the top of the cake, using a teaspoon or cocktail stick to ease the sauce down the sides in drips.

11. Decorate the top with caramel popcorn and serve straight away!

Tip: the caramel popcorn softens after being on the cake, so replace it with crunchy popcorn the next day (if you've got cake left).

SPECULOOS CHEESECAKE

Serves 8

Speculoos is an absolute must in my kitchen. I have to have a jar of the spread or a packet of the cookies in my cupboard—and it's all for the baking. This speculoos cheesecake is absolutely delicious and I'm sure you'll love it.

1. Prepare the springform pan by greasing and fully lining it with parchment paper. Then wrap the outside of the pan with two layers of thick foil, all the way up to the top edge. Preheat the oven to 325°F (160°C).

2. Crush the cookies to a fine crumb in a food processor (or place them in a bag and bash with a rolling pin). Place in a mixing bowl and then stir through the melted butter. Pour the crumbs into the base of the prepared pan and press down using the base of a glass until flat. Chill in the fridge while you make the cheesecake.

3. Grab the stand mixer (or a bowl and handheld electric whisk) and beat the cream cheese, cookie butter, flour, and light brown sugar together until combined, about 3–4 minutes.

4. In a small bowl, whisk together the eggs and sour cream until smooth and then slowly add this into the cream cheese mixture, stirring until creamy and lump free. Pour into the prepared pan and smooth out the top with a small spatula or the back of a spoon.

5. Place the pan into a large deep roasting pan in the oven and pour a kettle of boiling water into the roasting pan to surround the cheesecake and create a water bath. Bake the cheesecake for 1 hour 10 minutes, or until the edges are set and the middle is still slightly wobbly.

6. Once done, turn off the oven, put a wooden spoon in the oven door to hold it ajar, and leave the cheesecake in the oven until the oven cools down completely. Transfer the pan to the fridge overnight.

7. For the topping, melt 3½oz (100g) cookie butter in the microwave in 10-second bursts until it reaches drizzling consistency (about 30 seconds) and then flood the top of the cheesecake with it, allowing some to drip down the sides. Pop back in the fridge to set for about 30 minutes, then remove from the pan.

8. Whisk the whipping cream to stiff peaks and then swirl in the remaining cookie butter (you may want to loosen this for 15 seconds in the microwave). Pop into a piping bag fitted with a star nozzle and then pipe 8 rosettes or swirls around the top of the cheesecake. Stick a speculoos cookie onto each swirl or crush them over the top. Slice into eight pieces and serve.

FOR THE BASE

9oz (250g) speculoos cookies
5 tbsp (80g) unsalted butter, melted

FOR THE CHEESECAKE

1lb 5oz (600g) cream cheese
7oz (200g) smooth cookie butter
¼ cup (30g) all-purpose flour
½ cup plus 2 tbsp (120g) light brown sugar
4 large eggs
⅔ cup (150ml) sour cream

FOR THE TOPPING

7oz (200g) smooth cookie butter, divided
scant 1 cup (200ml) whipping cream
8 speculoos cookies

8 in (20 cm) springform pan
piping bag
star nozzle

MIXED BERRY CREAM PUFFS

Makes 12

You know when you eat something that just bursts with flavor in every bite? Well, this is that kind of bake.

1. Preheat the oven to 400°F (200°C).

2. In a small pan, gently heat the butter and ⅔ cup (150ml) water over medium heat until the butter has melted.

3. Add the flour all at once and beat well to incorporate. Cook for 2–4 minutes until it smells nutty and then remove from the heat and allow to cool to room temperature.

4. Using a stand mixer or handheld electric whisk, beat the eggs into the mixture, a little at a time, until you have a smooth, glossy paste that drops off the spoon easily.

5. Spoon the mixture into a piping bag fitted with a large round nozzle. Pipe 12 big dollops onto the two baking sheets, leaving a gap between them, and use a wet fingertip to press down any pastry poking up.

6. Bake for 15–20 minutes until cooked through and golden brown. Remove the puffs from the trays and cool on a wire rack. Poke a small hole in the bottom of each one with a knife to help the steam escape and keep them crisp!

7. Grab the pastry cream out of the fridge and whisk really well until creamy and light with a handheld electric whisk. Add the mixed berries to a blender and pulse until all blended. Pass through a sieve into the pastry cream and mix well to combine. Pop into a piping bag fitted with a star nozzle. Refrigerate again for 20 minutes or so.

8. To make the white chocolate glaze, put the chocolate into a bowl, then heat the cream in the microwave for 1–2 minutes until just below boiling. Pour over the chocolate and leave to stand for 2 minutes. Stir to create a smooth sauce.

9. Cut the puffs in half and pipe a swirl of berry pastry cream on the bottom half of each puff. Replace the tops and then drizzle with the glaze (or dip each top into the glaze to coat before adding it).

FOR THE CHOUX PASTRY

4 tbsp (60g) unsalted butter
½ cup (75g) white bread flour
2 large eggs, beaten

FOR THE PASTRY CREAM

1 batch Thick Vanilla Pastry Cream (see page 196), cooled
7oz (200g) mixed berries (I like raspberries, strawberries, and blackberries)

FOR THE WHITE CHOCOLATE GLAZE

5½oz (150g) white chocolate, roughly chopped
⅔ cup (150ml) whipping cream

2 piping bags
large round nozzle
2 baking sheets, lined
star nozzle

YUZU DAIQUIRI CHEESECAKE DESSERTS

Makes 4

FOR THE COOKIE BASE

5 tbsp (75g) unsalted butter
3¼ tbsp (40g) light brown sugar
1 tbsp grated fresh ginger
½ tsp vanilla paste
1¾oz (50g) honey
1 cup plus 2 tbsp (150g)
  all-purpose flour
1 tsp ground ginger
1 tsp baking soda
½ tsp salt

FOR THE CHEESECAKE

1¼ cups (300ml) whipping cream
9oz (250g) cream cheese
2 tbsp powdered sugar
grated zest of 1 lime
4 tbsp yuzu juice
4 tbsp white rum

TO DECORATE

1 batch Candied Lime Peel
  (see page 199)

4 glasses

You really don't have to faff around in the kitchen to make this one—serve in any glass you've got lying around or, even better, get your guests to build their own.

1. Make the candied lime peel the day before.

2. To make the cookie base, add the butter and light brown sugar to a pan over medium heat and let it melt and come together. Add the fresh ginger, vanilla paste, and honey to the pan and bring to a simmer.

3. Sift the flour, ground ginger, baking soda, and salt into a bowl and whisk. Continue to whisk as you add the butter and sugar mix and let come to a dough. Let cool slightly.

4. Roll out between two sheets of parchment paper to ¼ in (5 mm) thickness. Cut into two large cookies and place them on a baking sheet. Pop in the fridge.

5. Preheat the oven to 350°F (180°C).

6. Bake for 10–15 minutes, then leave to cool completely on the sheet.

7. To make the cheesecake mix, add all of the ingredients to a large bowl and whisk until soft peaks form. Pop the mixture into a piping bag and snip off the tip.

8. Crumble the cookie base into the bottom of the glasses. Pipe the cheesecake mixture evenly among the glasses and chill in the fridge for 2 hours, or until needed.

9. Add the candied lime peel on top just before serving.

BANOFFEE ECLAIRS

Makes 8

FOR THE FILLING

2 very ripe small bananas
1 batch Thick Vanilla Pastry
  Cream (see page 196), cooled
½ batch Caramel (see page 199,
  or make a whole batch and use
  the rest as a drizzle on some
  ice cream!), cooled

FOR THE CHOUX PASTRY

3½ tbsp (50g) unsalted butter
½ cup (75g) white bread flour
¼ tsp salt
2 large eggs, beaten

FOR THE GANACHE

2½oz (75g) dark chocolate,
  roughly chopped
⅔ cup (150ml) whipping cream

2 baking sheets, lined
2 large piping bags
large round nozzle

Banana and caramel is a combo that I'm obsessed with. Put it in a cake, a cookie, a pie, or an éclair—like here—and the results are always beautiful.

1. It is best to make the pastry cream and caramel for the filling the day before or the morning you'd like the éclairs, as these need time to cool, and éclairs are best served straight away with everything ready!

2. To make the choux, to a small saucepan add the butter and 6½ tablespoons (100ml) water and heat gently until the butter is melted. Bring to a boil and throw in all of the flour and salt. Beat well over low heat for a couple of minutes more until the mixture is stiff and sticks well to itself.

3. Remove from the heat and beat for a minute to allow the mixture to cool. Add the eggs, a little at a time, while you continue to beat. You may not need all of the egg, but as soon as the mixture gets to dropping consistency (it drops off the spatula nicely), then the mix is ready. Leave to cool.

4. Preheat the oven to 400°F (200°C).

5. Put the cooled choux pastry into a large piping bag fitted with a large round nozzle. Pipe eight éclairs about 5 in (12 cm) in length over the two lined baking sheets, leaving plenty of room between each one for them to puff up.

6. Bake for 20–25 minutes, or until dark golden brown.

7. When the éclairs are done, poke a couple of small holes in the bottom of each one to release the steam and then leave to cool on a wire rack.

8. Break the bananas into a bowl with the pastry cream and use a handheld electric whisk to mix them together until light and fluffy. Spoon into a piping bag and snip off the very tip.

9. Pipe the pastry cream into the éclairs through the small holes in the bottom, followed by some of the caramel (or you can slice the éclairs in half lengthwise and fill this way, if you prefer).

10. Make the ganache by adding the chopped chocolate to a bowl and heating the cream in a microwave for 1–2 minutes to just below boiling. Pour the hot cream over the chocolate and leave to stand for 2 minutes, before stirring to mix evenly.

11. Dip the éclairs in the ganache or drizzle over the top. Leave to set for 15 minutes before enjoying.

GIN & TONIC CHEESECAKE BITES

Makes 12

Cheesecake shot, anybody? Rock up to a party with these bad boys and everyone will be obsessed. They're the perfect bite-size treat. Eat them responsibly though, of course.

1. Start with the cheesecake bases. Crush the graham crackers finely either with a food processor or in a bag with a rolling pin. Mix with the melted butter and then press into the cupcake cases using a spoon or the bottom of a small glass. Pop in the fridge.

2. Add all of the cheesecake ingredients to a bowl and whisk well until thickened. Pop into a piping bag and snip off the tip.

3. Pipe the cheesecake filling into the cupcake liners and level with a teaspoon if needed, making sure the mixture goes to the edges properly so the jelly doesn't go down the sides. Return to the fridge for 1 hour.

4. To make the gin jellies, break the gelatin leaves into a small bowl, pour over 3½ tbsp (50ml) water, and leave to soak for 5 minutes.

5. To a pan, add the sugar, 6½ tablespoons (100ml) water, and all the citrus peels. Heat gently until fragrant and the sugar has dissolved (don't boil). Add the soaked gelatin leaves and their water, and stir to dissolve. Leave to cool to room temperature, then fish out the peels.

6. Add the gin, tonic water, and edible glitter, and then carefully pour over the cheesecake bites. Return to the fridge for at least 3 hours before serving.

FOR THE BASES

6oz (175g) graham crackers
5 tbsp (75g) unsalted
 butter, melted

FOR THE CHEESECAKE

scant 1 cup (200ml) whipping
 cream
6oz (175g) cream cheese
1½ tbsp powdered sugar
finely grated zest and juice of
 1 lemon

FOR THE GIN AND TONIC JELLIES

3 leaves platinum-grade gelatin
6 tbsp (75g) sugar
zest of 1 lime, peeled in strips
zest of 1 orange, peeled in strips
zest of 1 lemon, peeled in strips
½ cup (120ml) gin
6½ tbsp (100ml) tonic water
1 tsp silver edible glitter

*12-hole muffin pan, lined with
paper cases
piping bag*

PANCAKE PARTY

Makes 12

Invite your friends over for a pancake party and everyone can build their own. I've suggested cherries or berries to top your pancakes, but this recipe is all about having fun—I've given you the basics for making the perfect pancake, but the rest is up to you! This makes 12 pancakes, which is enough to serve four for brunch, but you can double the recipe for a larger gathering.

1. For the pancakes, start by separating the eggs. In a stand mixer (or mixing bowl with a handheld electric whisk), add the egg whites and whip until thick and fluffy and forming stiff peaks. Set aside.

2. Put the egg yolks in a separate bowl with the flour, baking powder, baking soda, salt, sugar, milk, and buttermilk. Whisk until combined and then drizzle in the melted butter with 2 tablespoons of the sprinkles. Fold in one-third of the egg whites to loosen the mix and then fold in the rest carefully, keeping as much air in as possible.

3. Heat a nonstick pan with a blob of butter and wipe around with a paper towel to remove the excess. Add a ladle of batter, add a few more sprinkles, and let cook for 2–3 minutes until bubbles appear all over the surface. Flip over and cook for another couple of minutes, and remove. Leave wrapped in a kitchen towel while you cook the rest of the pancakes.

4. To serve, whip the cream to soft peaks and fold the edible glitter through. Serve the pancakes, glittery cream, and cherries in the center of the table for everyone in the party to dig in!

FOR THE PANCAKES

4 large eggs
1¾ cups (225g) all-purpose flour
1½ tsp baking powder
1 tsp baking soda
¼ tsp salt
1 tbsp sugar
6½ tbsp (100ml) whole milk
½ cup (125ml) buttermilk
3½ tbsp (50g) unsalted butter,
  melted, plus extra for frying
4 tbsp candy sprinkles, divided

TO SERVE

2 cups (500ml) whipping cream
edible glitter
10½oz (300g) cherries, pitted,
  or other berries

MINI MANGO & ORANGE MERINGUE TARTS

Makes 12

These tropical tarts are packed with the sweetness of orange and mango, just like one of those smoothies you pick up on your way to work for a quick pick-me-up. Imagine taking one of these on your commute instead.

1. Make the pastry by popping all the ingredients except the water into a food processor, and pulse to make fine breadcrumbs. Slowly add the water, a tablespoon at a time, until the dough comes together. Turn out onto the work surface.

2. Bring the dough together gently and then roll out to about ¼ in (5 mm) thickness (it might be easier to do this in two pieces). Cut out 12 circles just larger than the tart pans, and then press the pastry circles into the pans. Pop in the fridge for 1–2 hours.

3. Preheat the oven to 400°F (200°C).

4. Line the pastry shells with parchment paper and then add baking weights into each one. Bake for 10 minutes and then remove the baking weights. Bake for another 10–15 minutes until cooked through and golden brown. Remove from the pans carefully and let cool completely on a wire rack.

5. To make the filling, add the diced mango, orange zest and juice, and the sugar to a saucepan. Over medium heat, gently stir to dissolve the sugar and then increase the heat to a simmer. Cook the mango pieces for 8–10 minutes until soft. Drain the mango pieces from the liquid and pop the liquid back in the pan. Add the eggs and yolk, and whisk to combine. Heat gently over medium heat, adding in the butter a few cubes at a time. Cook for 10–15 minutes over low heat to thicken, then pass through a sieve into a bowl. Add the mango pieces and set aside to cool.

6. For the Swiss meringue, pop a bowl over a pan of simmering water and add the egg whites and sugar. Mix together to combine and then heat gently until the sugar has dissolved—if you can no longer feel any sugar crystals, you're good to go.

7. Transfer the mixture to a stand mixer fitted with a whisk attachment and whip the egg whites until they are cool and super fluffy. Transfer this to a piping bag fitted with a large round nozzle.

8. Divide the cooled mango filling among the cooled tartlet cases.

9. Pipe the Swiss meringue on top of the tartlets in your preferred design and then toast with the blow torch.

FOR THE PASTRY

3½ cups (450g) all-purpose flour
1 cup (250g) unsalted butter, cold and cubed
2 tbsp sugar
2 large egg yolks
6–8 tbsp ice-cold water

FOR THE FILLING

2 mangoes, peeled and finely diced (about 1lb/450g)
finely grated zest of 1 orange
juice of ½ orange
½ cup (100g) sugar
2 large eggs
1 large egg yolk
6½ tbsp (100g) unsalted butter

FOR THE SWISS MERINGUE

6 large egg whites (about 6oz/180g)
1¼ cups (250g) sugar

12 tartlet pans
baking weights
piping bag
large round nozzle
cook's blow torch

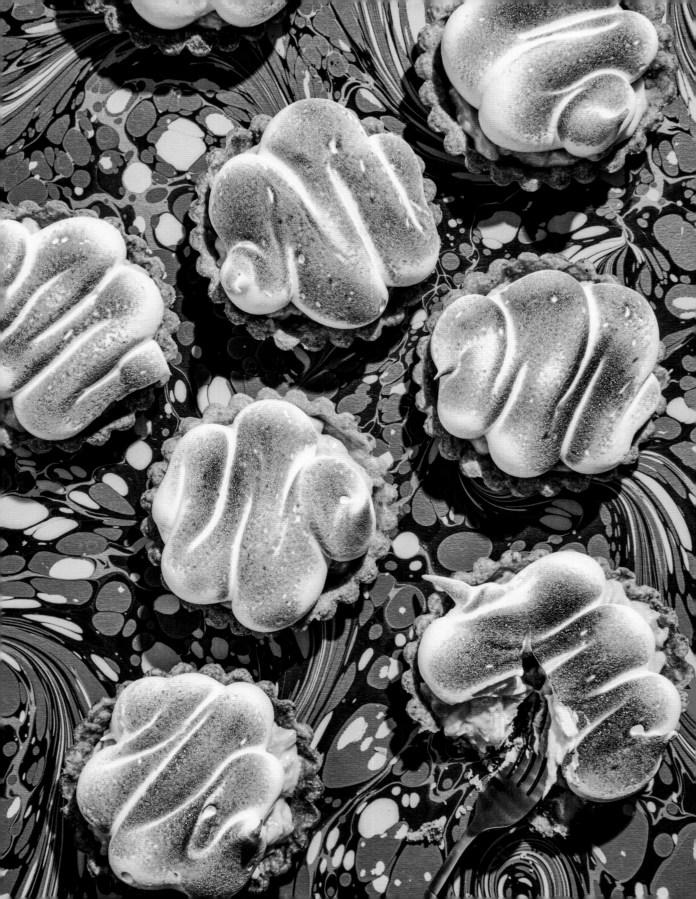

CHERRY HAND PIES

Makes 6

This is a good recipe to get children involved in baking. It's super-easy, fun, and very tasty. Fresh cherries are best here for a real summer picnic vibe.

1. In a large bowl, add the cherries, ½ cup (100g) sugar, 1 tablespoon cornstarch, and lemon zest and juice, and mix together.

2. Pop a colander or large sieve over another bowl and add the cherry mix. Leave for 10 minutes for some liquid to release.

3. Remove the pastry from the fridge about 10 minutes before you want to use it and then unroll. Cut both sheets into six equal triangles.

4. Toss the cherry mixture through the remaining cornstarch and then divide it between six of the pastry triangles, leaving a border around the edge. Brush some beaten egg around the edge and pop another pastry triangle on top. Use a fork to crimp the edges to seal.

5. Brush with more beaten egg and then sprinkle over with the remaining sugar. Place in the fridge or freezer for 20 minutes and preheat the oven to 375°F (190°C).

6. Pop the cherry pies in the oven for 20–25 minutes until crisp and serve warm with vanilla ice cream or whipped cream.

1lb 2oz (500g) fresh or frozen
  cherries, pitted and halved
  (defrosted if frozen)
¾ cup (150g) sugar, divided
2 tbsp cornstarch, divided
grated zest and juice of
  ½ small lemon
2 (11oz/320g) sheets
  puff pastry
1 large egg, beaten

LAYERED PAVLOVA CAKE

Serves 10

FOR THE HAZELNUT MERINGUE

5½oz (150g) hazelnuts
8 large egg whites (about
  10oz/290g)
½ tsp white wine vinegar or
  lemon juice
2 cups (400g) sugar

FOR THE POACHED PEACHES

6 peaches or 1lb 5oz (600g)
  frozen peach slices
2 cups (400g) sugar
2 tbsp vanilla paste
1¼ cups (300ml) dark rum

FOR THE WHIPPED CREAM

2½ cups (600ml) whipping cream
grated zest and juice of 1 lemon
scant ¾ cup (75g) powdered
  sugar
2 tbsp dark rum

TO DECORATE

edible flowers

2 baking sheets lined

I think a layered pavlova is the perfect centerpiece at any dinner, whether it's for a Christmas celebration or a summer party.

1. Preheat the oven to 400°F (200°C).

2. Add the hazelnuts to a baking sheet and roast for 5–8 minutes until golden brown. Use a clean kitchen towel to rub the skins off and then chop finely and leave to cool (leave some a little chunky for the top of the cake). Turn the oven down to 300°F (150°C).

3. Using an 8 in (20 cm) cake pan, draw four circles onto two sheets of parchment paper and then use the paper to line two large baking sheets, putting the paper pencil-side down.

4. In a stand mixer (cleaned with a little extra white wine vinegar or lemon juice), add the egg whites and white wine vinegar or lemon juice and start to whisk on medium speed for 5 minutes until frothy. Slowly increase the speed until you are on maximum and stiff peaks are achieved. Turn the speed down to medium and slowly add the sugar, a spoonful at a time, whisking until the meringue is super glossy and thick.

5. With a large metal spoon, fold through most of the hazelnuts. Spoon the meringue evenly among the four parchment circles, spreading to the edges evenly. On the fourth, have a little fun as this will be the top—swooshes and swirls all look great around the edge.

6. Bake the meringues for 45–60 minutes, or until pale brown all over and dry to the touch. Leave the meringues in the oven with it turned off and the door held open with a wooden spoon for a few hours until completely cool.

7. While the meringues chill out, let's make our rum-poached peaches. If using frozen peaches, skip this step, but for fresh, pop a large pan of water on to boil and prepare an ice bath. When the water is boiling, add the peaches for 1 minute and then transfer straight to the ice bath. Peel the peaches and remove the pits, then cut into wedges.

8. Reserve a scant 3 cups (700ml) of the peach boiling liquid in the same pan (or, if using frozen peach slices, add a scant 3 cups/700ml freshly boiled water to a large pan). Add the sugar, vanilla paste, and rum. Bring to a boil, reduce to a simmer, and then add the peaches. Poach until softened; this should take 6–8 minutes for fresh peaches or 2–3 minutes for frozen. Remove them with a slotted spoon and leave to cool on wire racks.

9. Reduce the rum syrup by half (this could take 15–20 minutes so be patient!) and then set aside.

10. In a large bowl, whisk the cream, lemon zest, and powdered sugar until you have soft peaks. Gently fold in the lemon juice and rum to combine.

11. Now you have everything ready, you can layer your pav! Start with a layer of meringue, add one-quarter of the cream, and then dunk the peaches into the reserved rum syrup before adding one-quarter of these, too. Repeat the layering process three more times and finish with the reserved crushed hazelnuts, any remaining syrup, and some gorgeous edible flowers.

SHARING IS CARING

This is what life is all about—sharing and caring.

I love making a cake, cutting it up and sharing it out in the community, whether it's with my neighbors or just people who need a little love out there. During the pandemic I started taking my bakes out into the community. The joy it brought to people—and myself, too—made me realize that food is the ultimate medicine. In this chapter are recipes that are made to be shared. Why not bake The Ultimate Orange Cake (see page 156) for mates, or share S'mores Cookie Bars (see page 149) with a neighbor. Of course, no judgment here if you decide to keep your bakes all to yourself. I mean, they are that good!

STRAWBERRIES & CREAM TIRAMISU

Serves 6–8

One of my all-time favorite desserts is a classic tiramisu, but I love the idea of combining it with the strawberries-and-cream flavor combination, so I made a tiramisu with strawberries instead of coffee. It's sweet, it's fresh, and it's perfect for spring and summer (but, let's be honest, you can make this dessert any time of year and nobody will judge you).

1. Start by making the strawberry coulis. Slice the strawberries in half if they're on the larger side and then pop in a pan with the sugar and lemon zest and juice. Heat gently over medium heat until the strawberries are completely broken down and the coulis is slightly thickened. Set aside to cool.

2. To make the tiramisu, in a large mixing bowl, add the cream, mascarpone, and cream cheese. Mix until combined and then sift in the powdered sugar and add the vanilla paste. Whisk until thickened.

3. Add the strawberry and cream liqueur to a small bowl and gently dip each ladyfinger in on both sides. Add a layer of soaked ladyfingers to the serving dish, followed by half of the cream and coulis. Use a vegetable peeler to shave off white chocolate shards from the bar. Repeat to make a second layer.

4. Decorate with some fresh strawberries, more white chocolate shavings, and sprigs of mint to garnish. Leave overnight in the fridge if you can, or for a minimum of 6 hours.

FOR THE COULIS

1lb 5oz (600g) strawberries, hulled
¾ cup (150g) sugar
zest and juice of ½ lemon

FOR THE TIRAMISU

scant 1 cup (200ml) whipping cream
9oz (250g) mascarpone
5½oz (150g) cream cheese
scant 1 cup (100g) powdered sugar
1 tbsp vanilla paste
scant 1 cup (200ml) strawberry and cream liqueur
32 ladyfingers (about 7oz/200g)
2½oz (75g) white chocolate

TO DECORATE

14oz (400g) strawberries
white chocolate
fresh mint sprigs

9½ x 6½ in (24 x 17cm) rectangular dish

COOKIE LAYERED CAKE

Serves 18

FOR THE COOKIES

1 cup plus 5 tbsp (300g) unsalted
  butter, softened
1½ cups (300g) sugar
2 large eggs
2 tsp vanilla bean paste
3¾ cups (500g) all-purpose flour
1½ tsp baking powder

FOR THE CREAM CHEESE ICING

1 cup plus 5 tbsp (300g) unsalted
  butter, softened
scant 6½ cups (800g) powdered
  sugar
14oz (400g) full-fat cream cheese

TO DECORATE

fresh fruits of your choice
edible flowers
edible glitter

4 square baking sheets, lined
piping bag
large round nozzle

If you are on Pinterest, you may have seen these cookie cakes and fancied giving them a go. Here's how.

1. Beat together the butter and sugar until smooth. Add the eggs and vanilla paste, and mix well until incorporated, then fold in the flour and baking powder. Bring it to a rough dough, cover in plastic wrap, and place in the fridge while you make the cream cheese icing.

2. To make the icing, beat the butter in a stand mixer fitted with a paddle attachment (or use a mixing bowl and handheld electric whisk) for 2–3 minutes until light and fluffy. Sift in the powdered sugar and beat for 3–4 minutes until smooth. Add the cream cheese and beat again for 2–3 minutes until combined—be careful not to over mix or the cream cheese will start to go runny. Pop into a piping bag fitted with a large round nozzle. Place in the fridge until ready to use.

3. Remove the dough from the fridge and roll it out to ¾ in (2 cm) thick. Use a dinner plate to cut out a circle and then use a smaller plate to cut out the middle, giving you a ring. Place the cookie dough ring on one of the lined baking sheets. Re-roll the dough to make another three rings.

4. Rest all the dough rings in the fridge for 30 minutes or in the freezer for 10 minutes. Meanwhile, preheat the oven to 375°F (190°C).

5. Bake the cookie rings for 12–15 minutes until golden around the edges and then allow them to cool on the baking sheets for 15 minutes before tipping out onto a wire cooling rack to cool completely.

6. Pipe little dots of icing onto the first ring and then top with the second ring. Do the same on the second and third layers, and then top with the final cookie ring. Finish the top in the same way and then add your toppings. I love a mix of seasonal fruit, edible flowers, and, of course, a bit of sparkle!

CARAMEL POACHED PEAR CRÊPES

Serves 4

FOR THE CRÈME ANGLAISE

1 cup (250ml) whipping cream
4 large egg yolks
¼ cup (50g) sugar
1 tbsp vanilla paste

FOR THE CARAMEL POACHED PEARS

2¼ cups (450g) light brown sugar,
   divided
3 cardamom pods, crushed
1 cinnamon stick, broken in half
1 vanilla pod, split lengthwise and
   the seeds scraped out
4 firm pears, peeled but stalks
   left on

FOR THE CRÊPES

1 cup (250ml) whole milk
scant 1 cup (200ml) whipping
   cream
3 large eggs
3½ tbsp (50g) unsalted butter,
   melted, plus extra for cooking
1½ cups (185g) all-purpose flour

Crêpes are so easy to make and these poached pears just take them to a new level. I could have this for breakfast or as a dessert—either way, it's perfect for sharing with others.

1. Let's start with our crème anglaise. In a small saucepan, heat the cream until the edges start to bubble. In a separate small bowl, whisk together the egg yolks and sugar until combined, and then pour the hot cream into them, whisking well. Pour this mixture back into the saucepan and add the vanilla paste. Heat over medium heat until thickened but still pourable, stirring constantly; this will take about 5 minutes. Add a layer of plastic wrap over the surface to stop a skin forming and set aside while we crack on with the pears and crêpes.

2. Add 1¼ cups (250g) of the light brown sugar, the cardamom, cinnamon, and vanilla seeds to a large saucepan with 3½ cups (800ml) water. Bring to a boil, then reduce to a simmer, add the pears, and then cover. Bubble away to poach the pears for 20–25 minutes, turning the pears over halfway through cooking. Test them by poking in a knife; if there's no resistance they are done.

3. Remove the pears carefully with a slotted spoon and transfer them to a bowl. Ladle out half of the poaching liquid and all the spices (add to the pears to keep them warm) and then add the remaining 1 cup (200g) brown sugar to the pan. Allow to bubble for 10–15 minutes to make a caramel sauce.

4. For the crêpes, use an immersion blender to whiz all of the ingredients up in a large bowl. (Or whisk the wet into the dry with a handheld electric whisk).

5. Pop a large skillet over medium heat. Rub the pan with a little butter and then ladle in enough batter to cover the center of the pan thinly. Roll it around so the batter reaches the edges and cook for 2–3 minutes on each side until golden. Wrap in foil to keep warm while you make the others (you should make 8 in total).

6. To serve, warm the crème anglaise through and then pour onto four plates. Fold the crêpes into quarters and place two on each plate. Add the pears and finish with a drizzle of the caramel sauce. Serve immediately!

PRALINE CUPCAKES

Makes 12

FOR THE CAKE

½ cup plus 4 tbsp (175g) unsalted
  butter, softened
¾ cup plus 2 tbsp (175g) light
  brown sugar
½ batch Caramel (see page 199),
  cooled and divided
3 large eggs
1⅓ cups (175g) all-purpose flour
1½ tsp baking powder
¼ tsp salt
3 tbsp milk

FOR THE PRALINE

3½oz (100g) blanched hazelnuts
1 cup (200g) sugar

FOR THE SWISS MERINGUE BUTTERCREAM

4oz (120g) egg whites
1 cup (200g) light brown sugar
1 cup (250g) unsalted butter,
  softened and cubed

*12-hole cupcake pan, lined
with paper cases
baking sheet, lined
piping bag*

Praline is such a nostalgic flavor for me. It takes me back to my childhood when my mum used to caramelize nuts in a pan of sugar. We would (impatiently) wait for it to cool down so we could tuck in.

1. Preheat the oven to 350°F (180°C).

2. For the cake, beat together the butter, light brown sugar, and 2 tablespoons of the caramel (reserve the rest for the buttercream) until super light and fluffy, about 4–5 minutes. Beat in the eggs, one at a time, and then fold in the flour, baking powder, and salt. Add the milk to make a nice dropping consistency.

3. Divide the batter among the cupcake cases and bake for 18–20 minutes until well-risen and a skewer inserted into the middle comes out clean.

4. Allow to cool in the pan for 10 minutes, before tipping out onto a wire rack to cool completely. Leave the oven on.

5. For the praline, add the hazelnuts to a baking sheet and cook in the oven for 8–10 minutes until golden brown. Leave to cool.

6. Add the sugar and 3 tablespoons water to a heavy-bottomed pan and heat over low heat until the sugar has dissolved. Increase the heat and bubble until a caramel is formed—it should be a dark amber color and start to smell really toasty!

7. Add the hazelnuts, stir quickly and then pour out onto the lined baking sheet. Leave to cool and harden fully.

8. For the Swiss meringue buttercream, add the egg whites and light brown sugar to a heatproof bowl over a pan of simmering water. Lightly whisk together and then heat gently until you can no longer feel the sugar crystals. Transfer to a stand mixer with a paddle or whisk attachment (or use a mixing bowl and handheld electric whisk) and whisk for 10 minutes, or until cool. Add the butter, one cube at a time, while whisking, then finish with 2 tablespoons of the reserved caramel and beat well to incorporate. Pop into a piping bag and snip off the tip.

9. Decorate the cupcakes with a swirl or a swoosh of the buttercream. Break the praline into pieces and place a piece on each cake. You can also whiz it up in a food processor, if you'd prefer a sprinkle!

S'MORES COOKIE BARS

Makes 8–10

I wouldn't class myself as a marshmallow fan, but I'm all about s'mores. This is a slightly less messy version, easy to make and easy to eat! No need to burn your fingers over a campfire here!

1. Preheat the oven to 375°F (190°C).

2. Beat the butter, sugar, and light brown sugar together until smooth and then add the egg and vanilla. Sift together the flour, baking soda, baking powder, and salt, then add to the butter and sugar mixture. Mix gently until a soft dough is formed.

3. Press half the cookie dough into the base of the prepared pan (it's easier to break off pieces and use damp fingers to smush them together) and then scatter over the graham crackers, half the chocolate chips, and 2oz (60g) of the mini marshmallows. Add the other half of the dough and then bake for 25–30 minutes until golden brown. Turn the oven off, and heat the broiler to high.

4. When the cookie comes out of the oven, scatter the remaining chocolate chips over followed by the remaining marshmallows to cover the top completely. Pop under the broiler for 30–45 seconds to toast them, then leave for at least 3 hours to cool completely in the pan.

5. Turn out and slice into bars with a sharp knife to slice through the toasty marshmallow! Finish with an extra sprinkle of graham cracker pieces.

½ cup plus 6 tbsp (200g) unsalted butter
½ cup plus 2 tbsp (130g) sugar
½ cup plus 2 tbsp (130g) light brown sugar
1 large egg, beaten
1 tsp vanilla paste
scant 2½ cups (320g) all-purpose flour
½ tsp baking soda
½ tsp baking powder
¼ tsp fine sea salt
1¾oz (50g) graham crackers, broken into pieces, plus extra to decorate
7oz (200g) milk or dark chocolate chips, divided
5½oz (160g) mini marshmallows, divided

8 in (20 cm) square cake pan, greased and lined

WHITE CHOCOLATE & LEMON CURD PAVLOVA

Serves 10

I can't have Christmas without a pavlova on the table. This is a perfect centerpiece; it is beautiful and tastes amazing. The tang from the lemon contrasts with the sweet meringue and white chocolate—it's a flavor combination that will have your guests coming back for seconds.

1. Make the lemon curd the night before so that it can set overnight.

2. Preheat the oven to 260°F (130°C).

3. Add the egg whites to a stand mixer fitted with a whisk attachment and start on medium-low speed (or use a mixing bowl and handheld electric whisk). Whip until soft peaks form.

4. Slowly add the sugar, one large spoon at a time, and continue whisking; it should take at least 3 minutes to add all the sugar. Continue to whisk on medium-low speed for 10–15 minutes until you can't feel any grains of sugar in the mix, and the meringue forms stiff peaks when the whisk is lifted.

5. Mix the cornstarch and lemon zest and juice in a small bowl until there are no lumps. Add to the meringue and whisk for 1 minute more.

6. Draw an 8 in (20 cm) circle onto parchment paper and place on a baking sheet (pencil-side down) using a bit of meringue dotted in the corners to hold it in place. Add the meringue to the circle to create a thick pavlova, using a spatula to create lots of height and make it about 3¼ in (8 cm) tall.

7. Pop into the oven for 30 minutes, then turn down the heat to 250°F (120°C) and cook for a further 45 minutes. Turn the oven off and leave the pavlova in there with the door open a crack (use a wooden spoon to keep it ajar) to cool completely for a few hours, or overnight if possible.

8. To make the white chocolate whipped ganache, add the white chocolate to the bowl of a stand mixer fitted with the whisk attachment (or use a mixing bowl and handheld electric whisk). Heat the whipping cream until just below boiling, then pour the cream over the chocolate. Leave it for 5 minutes, then gently whisk them together until smooth. Continue to whisk while it cools down. When at room temperature, add the vanilla paste and whisk on a high speed until thick—watch it like a hawk, because it can split quickly; but if it does, just drizzle in some extra whipping cream or cold milk.

9. To assemble, spread the whipped ganache over the pavlova base. Whip the whipping cream to soft peaks and swoosh it over the ganache to make lovely swoops. Drizzle over the lemon curd, making it as messy or as neat as you like! Dot the top with raspberries.

10. Make some chocolate curls with the white chocolate and a peeler. Finish with a few lemon peel spirals and serve to rapturous applause!

FOR THE MERINGUE

6 large egg whites (7½–7¾oz/ 215–220g)
1¾ cups plus 1 tbsp (360g) sugar
1 tbsp cornstarch
grated zest of 1 lemon
2 tsp (about ⅓oz/10g) lemon juice

FOR THE WHIPPED GANACHE

6oz (175g) white chocolate
scant 1 cup (200ml) whipping cream
1 tsp vanilla paste

TO ASSEMBLE

⅔ cup (150ml) whipping cream
1 batch Lemon Curd (see page 199; make this the night before so it sets)
7oz (200g) raspberries
1¾oz (50g) white chocolate
1 lemon, zested with a peeler to make spirals

1 baking sheet, lined

CARAMEL PASSION FRUIT CHEESECAKE

Serves 8–10

FOR THE CARAMEL

1 batch Caramel (see page 199)
pulp of 6 passion fruits (about
  2½oz/75g)

FOR THE CHEESECAKE

9oz (250g) graham crackers
½ cup (120g) unsalted butter,
  melted
1lb 2oz (500g) cream cheese
¾ cup (150g) sugar
grated zest of ½ lemon (about
  1 tsp)
pulp of 2 passion fruits, sieved
⅓ cup (50g) all-purpose flour
5 large eggs
6½ tbsp (100ml) whipping cream
1 tbsp cornstarch
6½ tbsp (100ml) dark rum

TO SERVE

pulp of 1–2 passion fruits

*8 in (20 cm) springform pan,
greased and lined on the base
with parchment paper*

This is the cheesecake of all cheesecakes. The passion fruit caramel is a huge hit, and combined with the creaminess of the cheesecake and the crunch of the case, it makes the ultimate treat. If you fancy making it a little sweeter just add more sugar to the cheesecake mixture

1. Make the caramel sauce according to the instructions on page 199, but add the passion fruit pulp when you add the whipping cream. Leave to cool completely.

2. Wrap the outside of the lined pan with two layers of thick foil, all the way up to the top edge.

3. Preheat the oven to 350°F (180°C).

4. Either in a sandwich bag with a rolling pin or in a food processor, crush the graham crackers until a fine crumb is formed. Mix with the melted butter and then press into the lined pan, all the way up the sides. Press well with a spatula around the pan to secure it as best you can and then pop in the fridge to chill.

5. In a mixing bowl, whisk together the cream cheese, sugar, lemon zest, passion fruit pulp, and flour until smooth. Whisk in the eggs, one at a time, and then add 3½oz (100g) of the passion fruit caramel, the whipping cream, cornstarch, and dark rum.

6. Pour the mix over the base and then add the pan to a larger roasting pan in the oven. Fill the roasting pan with boiling water so it comes halfway up the cheesecake pan. Bake for 55 minutes–1 hour until set around the edge but still a bit wobbly in the center. Turn the oven off and wedge the oven open slightly (use a wooden spoon to hold it ajar), and leave the cheesecake inside to cool completely; this will take 3–4 hours and helps stop a crack forming!

7. When the cheesecake has completely cooled, top the cheesecake with the remaining passion fruit caramel and some fresh passion fruit pulp.

EVERYTHING IN MY CUPBOARD SKILLET COOKIE

Serves 16

• SHARING IS CARING

FOR THE VANILLA ICE CREAM

2 cups (500ml) whipping cream
1 (13½oz/384ml) can sweetened
  condensed milk
pinch salt
1 vanilla pod, seeds scraped

FOR THE SKILLET COOKIE

½ cup plus 4 tbsp (175g) unsalted
  butter, softened
½ cup (100g) sugar
½ cup (100g) light brown sugar
1 large egg, beaten
1 tsp vanilla paste
2¼ cups (300g) all-purpose flour
½ cup (50g) unsweetened
  cocoa powder
¾ tsp baking powder
½ tsp baking soda
¼ tsp fine sea salt
1 batch Salted Caramel
  (see page 199)
9oz (250g) leftover chocolates
  (truffles, orange creams,
  pralines, etc.), roughly chopped

2 lb (900g) loaf pan
10 in (26 cm) skillet

Have you ever had one of those days when you just want to bake a cookie and it ends up being stuffed with everything in the kitchen, minus the kitchen sink? This is that cookie. You can stuff it with anything you have on hand and cook it in a skillet. All you need is ice cream and a spoon.

1. Let's start with the ice cream. Ideally you'd make this the day ahead! In a stand mixer with the whisk attachment or with a handheld electric whisk and large mixing bowl, add all the ingredients and whisk until stiff peaks form. Spoon into the loaf pan, cover with plastic wrap, and pop in the freezer for a minimum of 12 hours.

2. Preheat the oven to 400°F (200°C).

3. For the cookie, beat the butter, sugar, and light brown sugar together until smooth and then add the egg and vanilla paste. Sift together the flour, cocoa powder, baking powder, baking soda, and salt, then add to the butter and sugar. Mix gently until a soft dough is formed.

4. Divide the dough in half. Break off pieces of half of the dough and press into the bottom of the skillet. Drizzle over a layer of the salted caramel, reserving a few tablespoons for drizzling later, and then scatter over half of the chopped chocolates. Take chunks of the remaining cookie dough and flatten between your palms, laying them over the chocolate to create a top layer of cookie dough. Poke in the remaining chopped chocolates.

5. Bake for 20–25 minutes until cooked through and then serve warm in the skillet with the vanilla ice cream and the remaining salted caramel sauce drizzled over.

MARBLED BROWNIE & VANILLA COOKIE

Makes 12

I make these at least once a month, they just taste so good. The recipe combines a classic chocolate chip cookie with a brownie ... and the result is so satisfying.

1. Cream together the butter, sugar, and light brown sugar really well in a stand mixer fitted with a paddle attachment (or use a mixing bowl and handheld electric whisk) until smooth, about 4–5 minutes. Add the egg and vanilla paste and beat until smooth. Sift the flour, baking soda, and baking powder into the bowl and continue to beat until dough crumbs begin to form, about 20–30 seconds.

2. Divide the dough in half. Add the melted dark chocolate, cocoa powder, and the dark chocolate chunks to one half and the milk chocolate chips to the other half.

3. Split both doughs into 12 pieces, giving you 24 pieces in total. Roll each piece of vanilla dough with a piece of chocolate dough to make a swirly pattern. You should have 12 marbled cookies. Space them out evenly over the 2 baking sheets and pop in the fridge for 30 minutes or freezer for 15 minutes.

4. Preheat the oven to 350°F (180°C).

5. Bake for 12–15 minutes until they have spread and cooked through. Leave them to cool on the baking sheet for an hour before transferring onto a wire rack to cool completely.

½ cup plus 2 tbsp (150g) unsalted
  butter, softened
½ cup (100g) sugar
½ cup (100g) light brown sugar
1 large egg, beaten
1 tsp vanilla paste
2 cups (275g) all-purpose flour
½ tsp baking soda
½ tsp baking powder
1¾oz (50g) dark chocolate,
  melted and cooled
scant ¼ cup (20g) cocoa powder
1¾oz (50g) dark chocolate,
  broken into pieces
1¾oz (50g) milk chocolate chips

*2 baking sheets, greased
and lined*

THE ULTIMATE ORANGE CAKE

Serves 8-10

This is my mum's recipe. It is a simple cake that can brighten your day with its orangey flavor and light yet moist texture. It's perfect with a cup of tea! I grew up eating this cake and the smell of it baking in the oven on a Sunday morning brings back fond childhood memories. This is my take on my mum's delicious cake—I hope it can bring as much joy to your home!

1. Preheat the oven to 400°F (200°C).

2. In a stand mixer fitted with the paddle attachment (or using a mixing bowl and a handheld electric whisk), beat together the butter, sugar, and the finely grated orange zest until super light and fluffy, about 5 minutes. Add the eggs, one at a time, beating well between additions, adding a spoonful of the flour if it starts to curdle.

3. Sift in the flour, baking powder, baking soda, and salt, and fold through. Squeeze in the juice of one of the zested oranges to loosen the mixture slightly.

4. Pour into the prepared pan and bake for 30–35 minutes until it is risen, golden brown, and a skewer poked into the thickest part of the cake comes out clean.

5. Leave to cool in the pan for 10 minutes before turning out carefully onto a wire rack to cool completely. It shouldn't stick, but if it's taking its time, have patience! Gravity will work its magic as long as you've buttered the pan thickly and floured all the little nooks and crannies.

6. For the icing, add the orange zest and juice to a bowl and then sift in the powdered sugar. Beat well to make a smooth icing.

7. When the cake is cool, pop onto a serving plate and drizzle with the icing. Finish with the candied orange peels.

FOR THE CAKE

1 cup (230g) unsalted
  butter, softened
1 cup plus 2 tbsp (230g) sugar
grated zest of 2 oranges, juice of 1
4 large eggs
1¾ cups (230g) all-purpose flour
1 tsp baking powder
½ tsp baking soda
¼ tsp fine sea salt

FOR THE ORANGE ICING

grated zest and juice of 1 orange
scant 2 cups (200g) powdered
  sugar

TO DECORATE

1 batch Candied Orange Peel
  (see page 199)

*1 Bundt pan, buttered very well
and lightly floured (use melted
butter and a pastry brush for
super-detailed pans)*

BOLO DE GINGUBA

Serves 16

This sweet peanut-topped cake is a traditional Angolan recipe that is a favorite at parties and celebrations. It's a must-have in my family's Christmas dinners; in fact, pretty much every family occasion has this as a centerpiece. It is coated in caramel and topped with crunchy peanuts.

1. Preheat the oven to 350°F (180°C).

2. In a stand mixer fitted with the paddle attachment (or use a mixing bowl and handheld electric whisk), beat the margarine until pale. Beat in the sugar and 4 tablespoons of the caramel for a couple of minutes until the mixture gets light and fluffy. Add the eggs a couple at a time, beating well after each addition. If the mixture looks like it's splitting, add a spoonful of the flour.

3. Sift in the flour and baking powder, and fold through to make a smooth batter.

4. Divide the mixture between the prepared cake pans and bake for 30–35 minutes until well risen and a skewer inserted into the cakes comes out clean. Allow to cool in the pans for 10 minutes before turning out onto a wire cooling rack to cool completely.

5. If the cakes have domed slightly, cut the tops to level them and then spread a generous amount of the caramel on one cake and top it with the second one.

6. In the microwave, melt the remaining caramel slightly until a little more runny, then pour it over the top cake. Ease the caramel down the sides of the cake and use a spatula to ensure it's coated fully. Coat with the crushed peanuts.

2 cups (450g) margarine
2¼ cups (450g) sugar
1 batch Caramel (see page 199),
  cooled to room temperature
8 large eggs
3½ cups (450g) all-purpose flour
2 tsp baking powder
14oz (400g) roasted salted
  peanuts, crushed

*2 (10 in/25 cm) round cake
pans, greased and lined*

CRUNCHY CARAMEL CUPCAKES

Makes 12

FOR THE CAKE

½ cup plus 4 tbsp (175g) unsalted
  butter, softened
½ cup plus 2 tbsp (125g) dark
  brown sugar
¼ cup (50g) sugar
3 large eggs
scant ⅔ cup (60g) cocoa powder
scant 1 cup (125g) all-purpose
  flour
1 tsp baking powder
3–4 tbsp milk

FOR THE CRUNCHY CARAMEL GANACHE

3½oz (100g) milk chocolate,
  broken into pieces
7oz (200g) crunchy chocolate
  toffee bar, very finely chopped
scant 1 cup (225ml) whipping
  cream

TO DECORATE

mini crunchy chocolate toffee bars
gold dust

*12-hole muffin pan, lined with
paper cases*

Whenever I go to that famous Swedish home store, I always come
home with a big bag of toffee candy bars. I always plan to use them
for baking, but often end up eating them .... If you can resist eating
them first, have a go at these cupcakes.

1. Preheat the oven to 350°F (180°C).

2. Beat together the butter, dark brown sugar, and sugar until super light
    and fluffy, about 4–5 minutes. Beat the eggs in, one at a time, and then
    fold in the cocoa powder, flour, and baking powder in two halves. Add
    the milk to make a nice dropping consistency. Divide the mixture
    among the cupcake cases.

3. Bake for 18–20 minutes until well-risen and a skewer inserted into
    the middle comes out clean.

4. Allow to cool in the pan for 10 minutes, before turning out onto a wire
    rack to cool completely.

5. For the ganache, add the chocolate and chopped toffee bar to a bowl.
    Heat the cream in the microwave for 1–2 minutes until just below
    boiling. Pour the hot cream over the chocolate and leave to stand for 2
    minutes. Stir well to create a ganache and let cool to firm up.

6. Once cool, whip the ganache with a handheld electric whisk until
    thick. Spoon dollops of ganache on top of each cupcake, and then
    finish with a mini crunchy toffee bar and a spritz of gold dust.

BANANA PANCAKE BITES

Serves 2

These delicious little morsels will be gobbled up in moments. Top them with your favorite toppings and enjoy!

1. Slice the bananas into ½-in (1-cm) thick circles and set aside.

2. For the pancake batter, sift together the flour, protein powder, cinnamon, baking powder, and salt into a bowl. Make a well in the center and crack in the egg. Whisk the mixture together gently and then add the milk slowly to create the batter.

3. Heat a large nonstick skillet over medium heat and then brush with butter or oil. Dip the banana slices in the batter and then place carefully in the pan. Fry for about 2 minutes on each side.

4. Serve with a drizzle of your sweetener of choice, or your favorite fresh fruit with a dusting of powdered sugar.

FOR THE PANCAKE BITES

2 bananas
¾ cup (100g) all-purpose flour
1oz (30g) your favorite protein powder (or flour if you prefer)
1 tsp ground cinnamon
1 tsp baking powder
pinch salt
1 large egg, beaten
6½ tbsp (100ml) low fat milk or nondairy alternative
butter or vegetable oil, for frying

TO SERVE

agave or maple syrup
blueberries or other fruit
powdered sugar

CHOCOLATE HAZELNUT NO-CHURN ICE CREAM

Serves 10

Hazelnutty, chocolaty ice cream done the super-easy way!
No churning, no ice-cream maker, no hassle.

1. Preheat the oven to 400°F (200°C).

2. Add the hazelnuts to a baking sheet and roast for 6–8 minutes until golden brown. Leave to cool completely.

3. In a bowl use a handheld electric whisk to whip the whipping cream and sweetened condensed milk to soft peaks. Melt the chocolate hazelnut spread slightly in the microwave until more easily drizzle-able but not hot! Pour half into the bowl while whisking, along with the vanilla paste. Beat again to soft peaks.

4. Spoon one-third of the mixture into the loaf pan, drizzle with some more chocolate hazelnut spread, and add a sprinkle of the chopped hazelnuts. Repeat to create three layers, finishing with a chocolate hazelnut spread drizzle and some more chopped hazelnuts.

5. Cover with plastic wrap and freeze for at least 4 hours or overnight.

3½oz (100g) blanched hazelnuts, roughly chopped
2 cups (500ml) whipping cream
7oz (200g) sweetened condensed milk
14oz (400g) chocolate hazelnut spread
1 tbsp vanilla bean paste

2 lb (900g) loaf pan

MANY
HANDS

I remember baking with my mum as a child, and it's one of my fondest memories.

This chapter is all about getting together in the kitchen. Baking or cooking brings people together, so why not bring your child, sibling, flatmate, or whoever is in the kitchen with you? It's a bonding experience like no other. Some of the recipes in this chapter also form a little cheeky preview to my children's cookbook ... so I truly hope you enjoy it!

CHERRY BAKEWELL CRUMBLE BARS

Makes 16

This is one of my favorite bakes. It's the tang and sweetness of the cherries, the crunch and crumble of the topping, and the soft layer at the bottom—all three elements together are just mind blowing.

1. Preheat the oven to 350°F (180°C).

2. In a mixing bowl toss together the fresh or frozen cherries, the candied cherries, and the cornstarch.

3. In a separate bowl, mix the sugar, flour, ground almonds, oats, baking powder, baking soda, and almond extract. Using a fork or your fingertips, press the butter into the dry ingredients to make a rough crumbly mix.

4. Reserve a large handful of the crumble mixture and set aside.

5. Place the remaining crumble mixture into the cake pan and press slightly to compress. Spoon the cherry mix evenly on top, then scatter the reserved crumble randomly over the cherry mixture. Sprinkle over the flaked almonds and press in slightly.

6. Bake for 30–35 minutes until golden and crisp on top.

7. Leave to cool in the pan for 15 minutes, before turning out onto a wire cooling rack and letting cool completely.

8. Cut into bars and serve. (You can also serve this straight from the oven with cold whipping cream as a warm dessert!)

7oz (200g) fresh or frozen
  cherries, pitted and quartered
  (defrosted and drained if frozen)
3½oz (100g) candied cherries,
  halved
1 tsp cornstarch
½ cup plus 2 tbsp (125g) sugar
1 cup plus 2 tbsp (150g)
  all-purpose flour
1 cup (100g) ground almonds
½ cup (50g) rolled oats
½ tsp baking powder
½ tsp baking soda
½ tsp almond extract
½ cup plus 2 tbsp (150g) unsalted
  butter, chilled and cubed
1¼ cups (100g) flaked almonds

*8 in (20 cm) square pan, greased
and lined*

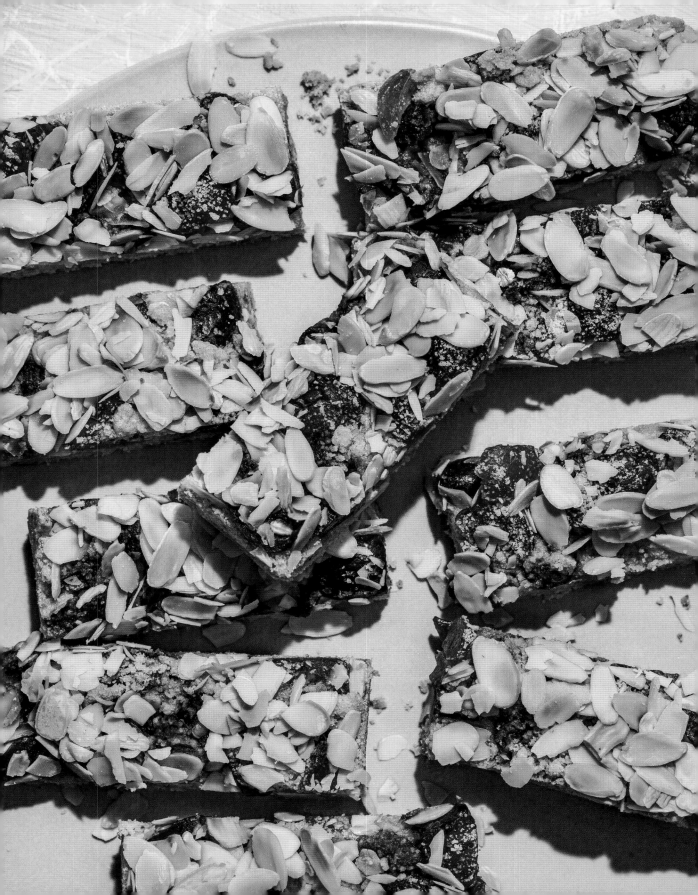

CARROT CAKE COOKIES

Makes 18

● MANY HANDS

FOR THE COOKIES

7oz (200g) carrots, coarsely grated
½ cup plus 4 tbsp (175g) unsalted
  butter, softened
½ cup (100g) sugar
½ cup (100g) light brown sugar
1 large egg, beaten
grated zest of 1 orange
1 tsp vanilla paste
2¾ cups (350g) all-purpose flour
1 tsp ground cinnamon, plus
  a little extra to decorate
¾ tsp baking powder
½ tsp baking soda
¼ tsp fine salt
4oz (120g) golden raisins
3½oz (100g) walnut pieces, plus
  extra to decorate

FOR THE TOPPING

3½ tbsp (50g) unsalted
  butter, softened
scant 1 cup (100g) powdered
  sugar, sifted
7oz (200g) cream cheese
1 tbsp orange juice (from the
  zested orange)

*2 baking sheets, greased
and lined*

This is a fun recipe to make with your children. It's really good for their motor skills—having to grate carrots and shape the cookies—and it's a great way to introduce vegetables in baking, making it that little bit healthier.

1. Squeeze out as much moisture as you can from the grated carrots with a clean kitchen towel. Spread them out on a chopping board or baking sheet and leave in a warm place for a couple of hours to dry further (or leave uncovered overnight in the fridge).

2. For the cookies, beat the butter, sugar, and light brown sugar together until smooth, and then add the egg, orange zest, and vanilla paste. Sift together the flour, cinnamon, baking powder, baking soda, and salt, then add to the butter and sugar. Mix gently until a soft dough is formed, then fold in the grated carrots, golden raisins, and walnuts.

3. Using an ice cream scoop, scoop out 18 cookies onto the baking sheet. Flatten the balls of cookie dough with your hand or the back of a spoon and refrigerate for 30 minutes.

4. Preheat the oven to 350°F (180°C).

5. Bake for 10–12 minutes until golden brown and set around the edges but still a bit soft in the middle. Leave to cool completely on the baking sheets.

6. While cooling, make the cream cheese frosting by beating the butter and sifted powdered sugar in a bowl until smooth and fluffy. Mix in the cream cheese and orange juice, and then leave in the fridge for an hour or until the cookies are completely cold.

7. Finish the cookies with a pillowy swoosh of frosting, a crumbling of walnuts, and a pinch of cinnamon.

MUM'S CLASSIC CARAMEL FLAN

Makes 10

Mum's flan is a classic for a reason and it's one for Christmas or any family gatherings. When I was young I loved watching my mum make this dessert, but I was too young to handle the hot caramel and help. I couldn't wait to be old enough, and now here I am!

1. Let's start by making the caramel. Spread the sugar evenly over the base of a medium saucepan, and gently pour in 2 tablespoons water. Place the pan over medium heat, and cook until the sugar has dissolved and becomes syrupy. Bring the sugar syrup to a simmer and cook until the color begins to change to golden amber and thickens, 5–7 minutes. Remove it from the heat and pour it into the flan pan, helping it coat all around the pan. Set aside.

2. Preheat the oven to 325°F (160°C).

3. Put the vanilla seeds and milk in a pan and bring it to a simmer.

4. In a separate bowl, mix the eggs, egg yolks, sugar, and sweetened condensed milk until well combined. Slowly pour the hot milk into the egg mixture while whisking constantly. Pour the custard through a sieve into the flan pan.

5. Place the flan pan inside a large roasting pan in the oven and fill the roasting pan with boiling water from the kettle to come halfway up the sides of the flan pan.

6. Bake the flan for 45–50 minutes until it is golden and feels firm yet wobbly when gently pressed. Allow to cool slightly, then refrigerate for at least 3 hours or overnight.

7. Turn out onto a large serving plate and slice—or dig in with spoons!

FOR THE CARAMEL

½ cup plus 2 tbsp (130g) sugar

FOR THE CUSTARD FILLING

1 vanilla pod, split and
  seeds scraped
1¾ cups (400ml) whole milk
2 large eggs
3 large egg yolks
½ cup (100g) sugar
6½ tbsp (100ml) sweetened
  condensed milk

9 in (22 cm) flan pan

COOKIE PIZZA

Serves 8

½ cup plus 4 tbsp (175g) salted
   butter, softened
½ cup (100g) sugar
½ cup (100g) light brown sugar
1 large egg, beaten
1 tsp vanilla paste
2¼ cups (300g) all-purpose flour
½ tsp baking soda
¾ tsp baking powder
¼ tsp salt
2½oz (75g) white chocolate,
   roughly chopped
2½oz (75g) milk chocolate,
   roughly chopped
2½oz (75g) dark chocolate,
   roughly chopped
1¾oz (50g) mini marshmallows
1¾oz (50g) pretzels, broken
   into pieces
1¾oz (50g) roasted hazelnuts,
   roughly chopped

*9 in (12 cm) springform pan,
greased and base lined with
parchment paper*

Cookies are just the best and this cookie pizza gives everyone a chance to be a part—top the slices with your favorites and it's the perfect recipe to share and make together.

1. Preheat the oven to 350°F (180°C).

2. In a large mixing bowl, beat the butter, sugar, and light brown sugar until lighter in color and creamy. Add the egg and vanilla paste, and mix well to incorporate.

3. In a separate bowl, sift together the flour, baking soda, baking powder, and salt, and then combine with the sugar and butter mixture to create to a dough, being careful not to over mix.

4. Fold in three-quarters of the chocolate chunks and marshmallows, along with all the pretzels and hazelnuts.

5. Press the cookie dough into the cake pan until the base is covered.

6. Bake for about 25 minutes until golden and cooked through.

7. While still warm, top with the remaining chocolate pieces and mini marshmallows.

8. Allow to cool in the pan for 15–20 minutes before scoring ten slice lines across the top—this allows for easy cutting later.

9. Let cool completely, then slice for an indulgent dessert, or allow to cool for 5 minutes in the pan, release carefully, and serve the slices warm with ice cream.

IRISH CREAM CUPCAKES

Makes 12

FOR THE PASTRY CREAM

1 cup (250ml) whole milk
scant 1 cup (200ml) Irish cream
6½ tbsp (85g) sugar
⅓ cup (50g) cornstarch
1 tbsp vanilla paste
4 large egg yolks
4 tbsp (55g) unsalted butter,
  chilled and cubed

FOR THE CUPCAKES

½ cup plus 4 tbsp (175g) unsalted
  butter, softened
¾ cup plus 2 tbsp (175g) sugar
1 tbsp vanilla paste
3 large eggs
1⅓ cups (175g) all-purpose flour
¼ tsp salt
1½ tsp baking powder
3½ tbsp (50ml) Irish cream

TO DECORATE

cocoa powder

*12-hole cupcake pan, lined
with paper cases
piping bag
nozzle of your choice*

If you know me and my baking, you will know that I use Irish cream liqueur a LOT! I love the flavor it brings. This isn't one for the children, but invite some friends over and bake these, not only will you have some fun but you will get a tasty bake in the end.

1. Start by making the pastry cream so it can cool. Heat the milk and Irish cream in a saucepan over medium heat until just below boiling.

2. In a large mixing bowl, whisk the sugar, cornstarch, vanilla paste, and egg yolks together until slightly thickened. Slowly pour over half of the milk mixture, whisk until combined, then add the second half.

3. Pour back into the saucepan and whisk until bubbling. Cook for a further couple of minutes until you can no longer taste the floury-ness of the cornstarch and the mixture has thickened and sticks to itself. Whisk through the butter and then pour into a bowl. Cover the surface with plastic wrap and leave to cool to room temperature, then pop in the fridge for 2–3 hours until cold. (You can speed up the cooling by pouring it out onto a tray!).

4. Preheat the oven to 350°F (180°C).

5. Beat together the butter, sugar, and vanilla paste until super light and fluffy, about 4–5 minutes. Beat in the eggs, one at a time, and then fold in the flour, salt, and baking powder. Add the Irish cream to make a nice dropping consistency.

6. Divide the batter among the cupcake cases.

7. Bake for 18–20 minutes until well risen and a skewer inserted into the middle comes out clean.

8. Allow to cool in the pan for 10 minutes, before turning out onto a wire rack to cool completely.

9. Take the pastry cream out of the fridge (and add to a bowl if you cooled it on a tray). With a handheld electric whisk, whip the cream until it's lighter in color and smooth. Add to a piping bag with your favorite nozzle.

10. Pipe the pastry cream on each cupcake in a design of your choice, and then dust with cocoa to finish.

PÉ DE MOLEQUE

Makes 20

This is a traditional treat in my culture—it's the sweetness and the crunch. These nutty caramel candy bites are similar to Florentines, but with a lot more crunch to them.

1. Preheat the oven to 350°F (180°C).

2. Spread the mixed nuts out on one of the lined baking sheets and toast for about 10 minutes until golden brown, turning halfway. Remove from the oven and leave to cool on the baking sheet.

3. In a medium heavy-bottomed saucepan, add the sugar, honey, corn syrup, and 6½ tablespoons (100ml) water, and place over medium heat. Cook until the sugar has dissolved. Bring the mixture to a boil, add the butter, and then cook for 15–18 minutes until the caramel is much darker.

4. Remove from the heat and add the baking soda, if using (it makes the final product a little softer and easier to eat).

5. Stir in the nuts and mix well. Pour the mixture onto another lined baking sheet and use the back of a metal spoon to spread the nutty mixture as thinly as possible.

6. Sprinkle the flaky salt on top and allow it to cool completely.

7. Once cool, break or cut it into bite-size pieces.

● MANY HANDS

12oz (350g) mixed nuts
2 cups (400g) sugar
1½ tsp honey
2 tsp light corn syrup
1½ tbsp (20g) unsalted butter
½ tsp baking soda (optional)
flaky sea salt

2 baking sheets, lined

CHOCOLATE & PISTACHIO PALMIERS

Makes 16

• MANY HANDS

FOR THE PALMIER PASTRY

2¾ cups (350g) all-purpose flour
1 tsp salt
1 cup (250g) unsalted butter, frozen
10–14 tbsp ice-cold water
1 cup (200g) sugar
3½oz (100g) pistachios, shelled to make 1¾oz (50g), then finely chopped

FOR THE TOPPING

scant 1 cup (200ml) whipping cream
3½oz (100g) dark chocolate, roughly chopped
3½oz (100g) pistachios, shelled to make 1¾oz (50g), then finely chopped

2 baking sheets, greased and lined

Making rough puff pastry for this recipe is where it all is. Palmiers are the pastry of all pastries for me. You can dip, drizzle, or even spoon some chocolate and pistachios on top, taking a classic to a new level. If you want to make a more classic palmier, don't add the pistachios to the rolled dough in step 3, and stop before adding the ganache and pistachios to the palmiers.

1. Start with the pastry by sifting the flour and salt into a large mixing bowl. Grate in the frozen butter using a coarse box grater and then gently toss the flour and butter together. Add the ice-cold water, a little at a time, and gently mix with a butter knife until a dough begins to form. At this stage squish together with your hands, being careful not to handle it too much, until a rough dough ball forms. Don't squish the butter in too much—you want to see streaks of it in the dough.

2. Flatten the dough into a rough rectangle, wrap in plastic wrap, and let it chill in the fridge for 30 minutes (or freezer for 15 minutes).

3. Once chilled, roll out the dough to a 8 x 12 in (20 x 30 cm) rectangle and fold into thirds, like a letter. Wrap it again and chill for another 15 minutes. Repeat this process twice more and the dough will begin to look smoother.

4. Now for the sugar! Repeat the same process as before twice more, but this time add half of the sugar on the pastry before you fold. With the final fold, sprinkle the insides with the remaining sugar and the pistachios.

5. On the last roll, roll out to a 16 x 10 in (40 x 25 cm) rectangle and mark the midpoint gently with a knife. Roll each side of pastry in toward the center to create the classic palmier shape. Chill for 15 minutes.

6. Cut into ½-in (1.5-cm) thick strips and place them cut-side down onto the lined baking sheets.

7. Chill in the fridge or freezer for 20–30 minutes and preheat the oven to 400°F (200°C).

8. Bake the palmiers for 8 minutes until golden, and then turn over and bake for a further 8 minutes. Leave to cool for 10 minutes on the baking sheets before transferring onto a wire cooling rack to cool completely.

9. For the topping, heat the cream in the microwave for 1 minute until just below boiling. Put the chocolate in a bowl and pour the hot cream over the chocolate. Leave for 2 minutes and then stir to create the ganache.

10. Drizzle the ganache over the palmiers using a spoon and add more pistachios over the top to finish. Leave to set for about 20 minutes before enjoying!

COCONUT & CHOCOLATE CAKE BARS

Makes 8

FOR THE CAKE

½ cup plus 4 tbsp (175g) unsalted
  butter, softened, or margarine
3½oz (100g) coconut cream
1 tsp coconut extract
1¼ cups plus 2 tbsp (275g) sugar
4 large eggs
2 cups (275g) all-purpose flour
1 tsp baking soda
2 tsp baking powder
½ tsp salt
5½oz (150g) dried, shredded
  coconut

FOR THE BUTTERCREAM

½ cup plus 6 tbsp (200g) butter
3¼ cups (400g) powdered sugar
2½oz (75g) coconut cream
splash coconut or dairy milk

FOR THE GANACHE

⅔ cup (150ml) whipping cream
3½oz (100g) dark chocolate,
  roughly chopped
1¾ tbsp (25g) unsalted butter

TO DECORATE

1¾oz (50g) white chocolate
handful toasted coconut flakes

*8 in (20 cm) square deep cake
pan, greased and lined*

I was inspired by coconut chocolates for this one and decided to make the flavor combination into cake—enjoy!

1. Start by preheating the oven to 400°F (200°C).

2. In a stand mixer fitted with the paddle attachment (or use a mixing bowl and handheld electric whisk), add the butter, coconut cream, coconut extract, and sugar. Beat well until light and fluffy. Add the eggs, one at a time, beating well after each addition. If the mixture starts to split, add a spoonful of the flour to get it back on track. Sift together the flour, baking soda, baking powder, and salt and fold this through in two batches. Add the dried shredded coconut and beat slowly to mix evenly.

3. Pour into the prepared cake pan and bake for 30–35 minutes, or until a skewer inserted into the middle comes out clean. Leave to cool in the pan for 15 minutes before turning out onto a wire cooling rack to cool completely.

4. Make the buttercream by beating the butter for 2 minutes on high until pale. Sift in the powdered sugar and beat again until light and fluffy. Add the coconut cream and a splash of milk if needed to adjust the consistency to a smooth buttercream. Pop into a piping bag and snip off the tip.

5. Line the cake pan again, but this time with a double layer of plastic wrap—two pieces going one way and another the opposite way so you can use the excess over the edge to help get the cake out.

6. When the cake is cool, slice off the top to level it out and then cut it horizontally into three layers.

7. Pop the first layer of cake into the pan and cover with one-third of the buttercream, spreading out to the very edge. Add another layer of cake and another layer of buttercream. Add the third cake and the rest of the buttercream. Press down gently to compact the layers, so you have a small amount of cake pan left at the top ready for the ganache.

8. Make the ganache by heating the cream in the microwave until just below boiling, about 1 minute. Put the chopped chocolate and butter into a bowl and pour the hot cream over the chopped chocolate and butter. Leave for 2 minutes, before stirring well to make a smooth ganache. Pour this over the final layer of cake, then pop it in the fridge for at least 3 hours.

9. Remove the cake from the pan carefully using the plastic wrap "handles" and trim each side with a warm knife to make smooth edges. Cut the cake in half and then each half into four; to make 8 bars.

10. To decorate, melt the white chocolate in a bowl in the microwave at 15-second intervals until smooth. Use a spoon to drizzle the white chocolate over the bars diagonally, and then sprinkle over the toasted coconut flakes.

PISTACHIO FLAPJACKS

Makes 9

Flapjacks are a perfect way to incorporate seeds, dried fruits, or nuts into your diet, and to introduce different foods to your children in a fun, healthy way.

1. Preheat the oven to 325°F (170°C).

2. Add the pistachios and oats to a food processor and pulse for a couple of minutes to create a chunky texture.

3. Heat the honey, maple syrup, and butter in the microwave or a small saucepan on medium heat for a minute or two to melt them together, and then stir into the pistachio and oat mixture, along with the salt and cranberries.

4. Press into the pan with the back of a spoon.

5. Bake for 20–25 minutes until golden brown at the edges. Leave to cool in the pan so they stay intact.

6. Once cool, remove and then slice into 9 squares.

7. Melt the chocolate in a heatproof bowl in the microwave at 30-second intervals until smooth. Drizzle over the squares and leave to set for 30 minutes before serving.

5½oz (150g) unsalted shelled pistachios
3½ cups (350g) old-fashioned oats
3 tbsp honey
3 tbsp maple syrup
3½ tbsp (50g) unsalted butter
½ tsp flaky sea salt
2½oz (75g) dried cranberries
3½oz (100g) white, milk, or dark chocolate

8 in (20 cm) square cake pan, greased and lined

LONG-PROVE LEMON-GLAZED RING DOUGHNUTS

Makes 12

Frying these is all about the oil—the key is to get the temperature of the oil just right and then it'll make the doughnuts just right. This is definitely one to bake together—kneading the bread dough is therapeutic and it's just a bit of fun to make. The only issue is once you know how to make it, the obsession begins!

1. In a small bowl microwave the milk and butter until the butter has melted and the milk is slightly warm.

2. Add the flour, sugar, yeast, and lemon zest to a stand mixer fitted with a dough hook (or a mixing bowl) and make a well in the center. Add the warmed milk mixture and start to combine slowly. When combined, add the egg, and then knead for 8–10 minutes until a soft dough forms that springs back when poked. Cover with plastic wrap and pop in the fridge overnight or for at least 8 hours.

3. In the morning, take the dough out of the fridge and turn it out onto a floured worktop. Roll out gently to a large rectangle.

4. Cut out 12 large circles and then cut out the centers using the smaller cutter. You can re-roll the dough, if you like, but these might not rise as much as the first batch!

5. Leave them to prove on a floured baking sheet, covered with greased plastic wrap, for another hour at room temperature.

6. Heat up the oil in a large saucepan to 320°F (160°C). You should have enough oil that your doughnuts can float. Fry 2–3 doughnuts at a time, flipping them over after a minute, or when golden brown.

7. Drain on a cooling rack and then mix together the lemon juice and powdered sugar to make a glaze. Drizzle the glaze over the doughnuts or dip them into it. Leave to set for a few minutes, if you can wait that long!

8. If you like, mix the sugar and cinnamon together and sprinkle this over the tops.

1¾ cups (140ml) whole milk
3½ tbsp (50g) unsalted butter
3 cups (350g) white bread flour,
   plus extra for dusting
1¾ tbsp (20g) sugar
1 (¼oz/7g) packet fast acting
   dried yeast
grated zest and juice of
   1 large lemon
1 large egg, beaten
vegetable oil for frying
1 scant cup (100g) powdered
   sugar
¼ cup (50g) sugar (optional)
1 tsp ground cinnamon (optional)

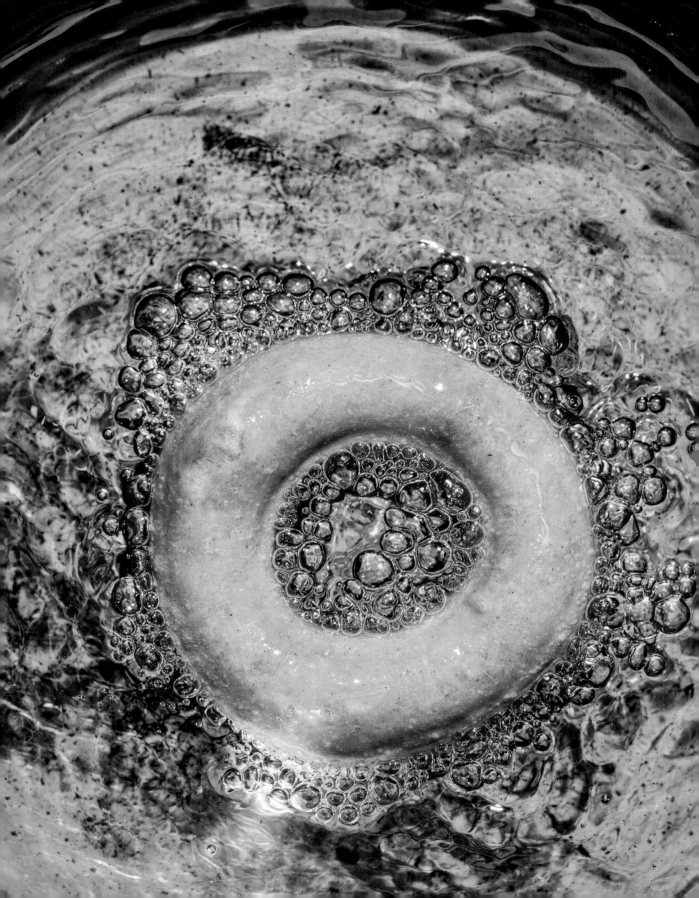

BASIC RECIPES & TECHIQUES

The secrets to success

I often get asked for my buttercream recipe, and how to make caramel, and I want to say—I hear you! Here you'll find the basic recipes that are used throughout the book, as well as some instructions for cake stacking, crumb-coating, and frosting, and tips for that iconic drip decoration. These are the principles for any good baker and they're easy to learn. Why not keep them up your sleeve or make them your own for any of your own bakes, too?
You can thank me later!

LEVELING & STACKING CAKES

To make a cake stand straight you need to level the layers, before stacking them. This involves removing the domed top of the cake to ensure it's level. A common mistake is to use the filling to try to make a stacked cake stand up straight, but eventually this will make the cake lopsided. You want to make sure that each layer of cake is as even as possible.

Use a cake-leveling tool, if you can find one. They are easy to use and guarantee you a level cake. However, I like using my long serrated cake knife; it is one of my must-have tools. Using a serrated knife and a turntable allows me to remove less cake, meaning less waste (although the leveling tools are good, you have to cut a good chunk for it to work).

To prepare the cake layers, I start by placing one cake on a turntable. I carefully remove the caramelization from the bottom and top of the cake. Repeat for the other layers.

If you need to cut the cake in half horizontally, score the middle of the cake while spinning the turntable, then gently start cutting through the cake until you have cut it in half to create two layers.

Once you have leveled each layer, you can stack the cakes, adding the buttercream or filling between each layer.

CRUMB-COATING CAKES

I use an offset spatula, a cake scraper, and my buttercream (see page 196) to stick any loose crumbs onto the cake, spreading a thin layer of buttercream all over the outside of the cake.

Place the cake in the fridge or freezer for about 30 minutes until the crumb coat is firm to the touch. This is your base layer of frosting before the outer layer that you will decorate.

FROSTING CAKES

For a perfectly smooth frosting, I place a second cake board (the same size as the cake board the cake is on) on top of the cake and make sure it's aligned with the one at the bottom. Using a palette knife or cake scraper, I go around with the frosting, making sure the cakes have an equal frost all around. Remove the cake board from the top of the cake and use a warm small offset spatula to neaten the edges by carefully going over it.

PERFECT ROUND COOKIES

Don't you hate when your cookies just spread too much? I would eat them even with the spread, but I do love a perfectly round cookie and it is so easy to get them. As soon as you remove the cookies from the oven, place a round cookie cutter that's slightly larger than the cookie over each cookie, and use a circular motion to bring them back to a perfect circle (you've got to do this while they're still warm; if they've hardened just pop them back in the oven for a few minutes and try again).

It's also important not to overcrowd your baking sheet, so if they spread, you can easily bring each cookie into a perfect circle and they won't stick to each other.

CHOCOLATE DRIPS

The main thing you need to do is make sure your cake has a smooth frost and has chilled in the fridge overnight (you can also pop your cake in the freezer for about 15–20 minutes if you're in a hurry). Make sure the chocolate ganache has cooled and isn't hot to touch—you want it to drip, but not be runny, so give a test on the edge of a bowl and see how it drips down.

Use a piping bag or a squeezy bottle for precision, or a small spoon to slowly go over the edges of the cake with the chocolate sauce, one drip at a time, while spinning the turntable. Return the cake to the fridge to stop the drips from over-dripping.

VANILLA PASTRY CREAM

2¼ cups (550ml) whole milk
½ cup (100g) sugar
¼ cup (40g) cornstarch
1 tbsp vanilla paste
4 extra large egg yolks
4 tbsp (55g) unsalted butter, cold and cubed (optional)

1. Heat the milk in a pan over medium heat until just below boiling.

2. In a large mixing bowl, whisk the sugar, cornstarch, vanilla paste, and egg yolks together until slightly thickened. Slowly pour over the hot milk and whisk until combined.

3. Pour back into the pan and whisk until bubbling. Cook for a couple of minutes until you can no longer taste the cornstarch and the mixture has thickened. Whisk through the butter for an extra rich taste.

4. Pour into a bowl (or tray to cool quickly). Cover with plastic wrap, let cool to room temperature, then chill for 3–4 hours to thicken.

Tip: for Thick Vanilla Pastry Cream, reduce the sugar to 6½ tbsp (85g) and increase the cornstarch to a scant ⅓ cup (50g).

VANILLA BUTTERCREAM

1lb (450g) unsalted butter, softened
7½ cups (900g) powdered sugar, sifted
2 tbsp vanilla paste
3–4 tbsp milk

1. Beat the butter until pale and fluffy in a stand mixer fitted with a paddle attachment, about 2 minutes. Use a silicone spatula to wipe round the sides of the bowl and bring the butter back into the middle.

2. Add the powdered sugar in batches, and then add the vanilla paste (or any other flavoring) and beat for 3–5 minutes until super white.

3. Slowly add the milk until you reach the correct consistency. Cover and leave at room temperature until needed.

Tip: for the perfect buttercream frosting, use unsalted block butter (not margarine) at room temperature.

Make sure to sift the powdered sugar to ensure there are no lumps.

I always recommend using a vanilla bean paste, especially if you're not using food coloring.

SWISS MERINGUE BUTTERCREAM

8½oz (240g) egg whites
2 cups (400g) sugar
2 cups plus 2 tbsp (500g) unsalted butter, softened and cubed
2 tbsp vanilla paste

1. Add the egg whites and sugar to a heatproof bowl over a simmering pan of water. Lightly whisk together and then heat gently until you can no longer feel the sugar crystals between your fingers.

2. Transfer to a stand mixer with a paddle or whisk attachment and whisk for 10 minutes or until cool to the touch. Add the butter, one cube at a time. The mixture might look soupy or like it's seizing, but persevere!

3. Finish by whipping through the vanilla paste.

Tip: the trick with Swiss meringue buttercream is usually temperature. If it doesn't seem right, try refrigerating for a bit and then beating again or warming the bowl gently with a warm towel.

CANDIED CITRUS PEELS

2 limes, 1 orange, or 1 lemon
1¼ cup (250g) sugar

1. Start by slicing your citrus into wedges and then use a small paring knife to carefully cut the flesh from the skins. Scrape the white pith off the peels and then slice into thin strips. Squeeze the juice from the remaining wedges into a pan and add 1¾ cups (400ml) water.

2. Bring to a simmer, cover, and add the strips. Cover and cook for 20–25 minutes until soft (for thicker strips, this may take a bit longer).

3. Use tongs to remove the peels. Pour the citrusy water into a measuring cup. Top up to a scant 1 cup (200ml) with hot water if you need to. Add back into the pan with ¾ cup (150g) sugar. Bring to a boil and add the peels back into the syrup. Cook for 25 minutes until translucent. Remove and let dry on a wire rack for 24 hours.

4. When dried out, toss in the remaining sugar to coat.

LEMON CURD

finely grated zest and juice
  of 3 lemons
3 extra large eggs
½ cup (100g) sugar
pinch salt
5 tbsp (75g) unsalted butter, cubed

1. In a heavy-bottomed saucepan, add the lemon zest and juice, eggs, sugar, and salt. Whisk together until the sugar has dissolved and the mixture is frothy.

2. Pop over medium heat and add the butter. Use a rubber spatula to stir constantly until the liquid releases a few bubbles.

3. Remove and transfer to a jar immediately and screw on the lid. Cool to room temperature and then pop in the fridge. (You can also pass your curd through a sieve before this stage if you see any little lumps!)

CARAMEL

1½ cups (300g) sugar
⅔ cup (150ml) whipping cream
6½ tbsp (100g) unsalted butter

1. In a medium light-colored pan, stir together the sugar and ¼ cup (60ml) water to begin to let the sugar dissolve. Place over low heat and swirl around until the sugar is completely melted, making sure not to stir.

2. Increase the heat and bubble until a dark amber caramel is formed—almost smoking gives great flavor!

3. Turn the heat down to low. Add the cream and stand back in case it bubbles up, then mix well until fully combined. Next, add the butter and stir constantly until melted and mixed.

4. Leave to cool in a jar, or let cool to barely warm, then transfer to a container with a lid.

Tip: for Salted Caramel, add 1 tsp salt at the end of step 3.

INDEX

Thanks

So, that was my first ever cookbook! I hope you enjoyed it as much as I enjoyed creating this for you all.

It means the world to me to have been able to do this and with such a great team, I want to end by just thanking a few people.

Firstly, I want to thank my mother. If she didn't bake during those weekends when I was younger, I may have never found the love of baking, and the support my mum gives me is beyond—I know it's all possible.

Secondly, I want to thank my partner who always pushes me and makes me better. The love is truly unconditional and it's why I can have the courage to create something like this.

I also want to thank my amazing management team who has been on my side throughout the making of the book and have been truly amazing to me, love you MKB.

I want to also thank DK who believed in me enough to offer me this opportunity. They have been so patient and so supportive, and I couldn't think of a better publishing house. Thank you DK and especially, Cara, Izzy, Barbara. Thank you to the whole team: Dom, Daisy, Liz and Max, Nikki, Emma, Kate, and everyone involved in my book, I'm truly grateful.

And lastly I want to thank you, I want to thank you for buying this book to start with and for supporting me throughout. You guys are truly the best, I couldn't ask for better support, it truly makes me feel warm and brings tears of joy knowing that I am supported by so many, so thank you.

About the Author

Sandro Farmhouse won the hearts of millions during his appearance on *The Great British Baking Show (The Great British Bake Off)* in 2022, where he made it to the final and came second.

Now a full-time baker, he has a popular Instagram account and makes regular appearances on ITV's *This Morning* and *Lorraine*, as well as Channel 4's *Steph's Packed Lunch*. Sandro's skills have led him to bake for stars including Stormzy and Little Mix. Before appearing on our screens, Sandro worked as a nanny and has since founded "Baking on the Spectrum"—an online workshop and resource that aims to create an inclusive and safe space for neurodiverse children and their caregivers to engage with baking as sensory play. *Good Vibes Baking* is his first book.

Editorial Director Cara Armstrong
Project Editor Izzy Holton
Senior US Editor Megan Douglass
US Consultant Renee Wilmeth
Senior Designer Barbara Zuniga
Production Editor David Almond
Production Controller Samantha Cross
DTP and Design Coordinator Heather Blagden
Jacket and Sales Material Co-ordinator Emily Cannings
Art Director Maxine Pedliham
Publishing Director Katie Cowan

Editorial Kate Reeves-Brown
Design Nic & Lou
Photography Haarala Hamilton
Prop styling Daisy Shayler-Webb
Food styling Dominique Eloïse Alexander

First American Edition, 2024
Published in the United States by DK Publishing
a division of Penguin Random House LLC
1745 Broadway, 20th Floor, New York, NY 10019

Text copyright © 2024 Sandro Farmhouse
Photography copyright © 2024 Haarala Hamilton
Copyright © 2024 Dorling Kindersley Limited

Sandro Farmhouse has asserted his right to be
identified as the author of this work.

24 25 26 27 28 10 9 8 7 6 5 4 3 2 1
001–339284–May/2024

A catalog record for this book
is available from the Library of Congress.
ISBN: 978-0-7440-9418-3

Printed and bound in Latvia

www.dk.com

This book was made with Forest
Stewardship Council™ certified
paper—one small step in DK's
commitment to a sustainable future.
Learn more at **www.dk.com/uk/
information/sustainability**

PUBLISHER'S ACKNOWLEDGMENTS

DK would like to thank Sarah Epton for
proofreading, Lisa Footitt for indexing,
and Adam Brackenbury for the image
retouching. Thank you to Lucy Cottle,
Alice Katie Hughes, Izy Hossack, Bea
Turner, and Archie Montgomery for their
help with food styling, Sandra for her
wonderful soups, and Stuart Alexander
for the homegrown rhubarb. Thanks as
well to Pushpak Tyagi for his design support.